UNCOMMON RELATIONSHIPS:
Bringing Healing and Joy to Our Christian Experience

By

Robert D. Kuest

New Mission Systems International
Fort Myers, Florida

DEDICATION

To

Dean, David, Sheila and Scott

Four wonderful gifts from God

with whom Peggy and I

enjoy uncommon relationships

TABLE OF CONTENTS

ACKNOWLEDGEMENTS

An author gets credit for writing a book; however, no author ever wrote a book without a cadre of people in the background. *Uncommon Relationships* is no exception to that truth. There are many who listened to these three lessons and encouraged me to put them into writing. I am grateful to my friend Ron Kuest who gave me my first copy of *Leadership and Self-Deception* from which the second chapter of this book emerged. I have appreciated the input and advice given by James Fuller, C.E.O. of the Arbinger Institute, as well as the permission to use extensive quotes and references from their two books – *Leadership and Self-Deception* and *The Anatomy of Peace*.

The task of writing can only be accomplished with the help of others. An author knows that they themselves are the worst proof-readers of their own work. Therefore, I have leaned upon my wife and my friend, Ray Runkle, to help with this matter.

I am not an artist, however, Phil Barrera is a very gifted friend who took my abstract thinking and created the beautiful cover for this book.

Behind my wife and I stand about 200 Prayer Partners who hold us up before the Lord on a regular basis. Their intercession brings forth God's energy for our ministry, whether speaking or writing. We are convinced that without them none of this would be possible.

Thank you to all,

Bob

So from now on we regard no one from a worldly point of view. Though we once regarded Christ in this way, we do so no longer. Therefore, if anyone is in Christ, he is a new creation; the old has gone, the new has come! All this is from God, who reconciled us to himself through Christ and gave us the ministry of reconciliation: that God was reconciling the world to himself in Christ, not counting men's sins against them. And he has committed to us the message of reconciliation. We are therefore Christ's ambassadors, as though God were making his appeal through us.

~~2 Corinthians 5:16 - 20

UNCOMMON RELATIONSHIPS:
Bringing Healing and Joy to Our Christian Experience
By
Robert D. Kuest

INTRODUCTION

Over forty years as a leader in church and missions has taught me that God's principles bring true satisfaction for which many hearts are seeking. His guidelines for living transcend time and culture; and are just as valid today as they were when given to inspired biblical writers. God's ways, however, are not the norm for most people, in any culture. Every ethnic group has its own definition of *fame, fortune* and *power* as life-goals. Each produces the same emptiness and brokenness where life really counts – relationships. Therefore, when a person or a group is discovered to be enjoying life-fulfillment through God's higher way of thinking (Is 55:8-9), observers evaluate their actions as *uncommon*, not the way people normally live.

My wife and I work in many countries with people in many different life situations. We are often asked, "How can you experience success in every venue?" We have found a one word answer. <u>The key to success in families, churches and businesses is *relationships.*</u> There have been thousands of *how to* books written covering every conceivable area of life. However, no book dealing with people (marriage, business, leadership, etc) will work without understanding what happens in relationships – how they grow, what strains them and what strengthens and maintains them.

The most successful teachings in any form will point us to God's principles for relationship. Following His example and teachings will provide us with deep satisfying relationships that lead to success in marriage and leadership. These principles are not only for individuals; if the Church, as the Body of Christ, would apply these principles it could revolutionize our impact on a community. Hopefully, this short series of three lessons can provide some understanding that will help the reader experience *uncommon relationships*.

Like everyone else on this planet, I have experienced relationship problems. During one of these strained times, I shared the troubling situation with our good friend and colleague Ron Kuest (no relation that we can trace). Instead of *counseling* (or *consoling*) me in the relationship, he said, "I have a book I want you to read." That was not the answer I really wanted to hear. He gave me a copy of *Leadership and Self-Deception* and simply said, "Please read this."

This book made a dramatic impact on my life and thinking. So much so, I wanted to start teaching about relationships in our travels around the world.

However, I had two problems to solve before I could develop lessons. First, in both books published by the Arbinger Institute, *Leadership and Self Deception* and *Anatomy of Peace* (a prequel published after the first book), the authors use an illustration of us "being in a box when we think and act selfishly." It is a good illustration; however, it would not translate in most foreign cultures where we teach. Second, I felt the principles suggested in these books parallel scripture and I wanted to fuse the two together. So I started praying and making notes. The metaphor of the box remained a problem; how do you explain the concept of "being *in* or *out* of a box" to people in very literal cultures?

I remembered in February 2000, I tried to preach in Renigunta, India, a small town about two hours north of Chennai. I described a long-distance runner reaching the point where he feels he can go no farther. Runners call this feeling of exhaustion, "hitting the wall." My translator translated the words and then turned to me and asked, "What does that mean?" He could only picture a man hitting a wall with his fist and it made no sense to what I was saying in the sermon. I tried to explain but he could not understand. I told him, "Let's go on with the message." He would not go on. He kept pushing for further explanation so he could tell the people about "hitting the wall." For more than ten minutes he questioned me while people sat and I tried (futilely) to explain. When I thought of teaching about "being *in* or *out* of a box," the frustrating memories of that day came flooding back.

As I was beginning to put my thoughts together on how to teach *relational* concepts in different cultures, I happened to visit a small cultural museum in Kitale, Kenya. In the museum we came upon a life-sized diorama of an ancient Luou village. Suddenly I was face-to-face with a warrior with his shield and sword raised. As I looked at that man posed for battle, I realized that I had found an illustration that would translate anywhere in the world. Raising a *shield* to protect our being would represent us being "in the box." Lowering our *shield* to become vulnerable would equal "out of the box." The sword would represent our deflecting blame to another person or source. This metaphor approximates the idea expressed by The Arbinger Institute in *The Anatomy of Peace* that our hearts can either be at war or at peace toward one another.

Our subject for these lessons is *relationships* and how they affect our families, our church and our leadership. So many times these relationships are damaged because we so quickly take a defensive posture when we feel threatened by someone's words and/or actions. We, like a warrior in battle, immediately raise a shield (mental, rather than physical) and grab a sword (usually a pointed-finger) to attack or blame. Instead of protecting relationships, we injure them.

"Life is relationships; everything else is just details." This quote begins Author/speaker Gary Smalley's book, The DNA of Relationships. He goes on, "Everything in life that truly matters can be boiled down to relationships."[1] Relationships begin when we see people as significant; someone with whom we would like to associate. They end when we pass judgment and no longer accept their worth.

The possibilities for creating and healing relationships best happen when I accept a person's worth by learning to see them through God's eyes. I will discuss this in the first lesson. However, Satan opposes any type of positive relationship. His goal from the Garden of Eden to the present has been to separate relationships and leave people with the emptiness of feeling alone.

When I experience a strained relationship something inside me tries to convince me that I must fight to prove or hold on to my significance. I have seen this same reaction all around the globe. Not only have I have seen it in individuals, but also in churches and mission organizations. In every interpersonal transaction, people stand ready with a mental shield and sword to protect themselves. However, choosing the wrong protection can lead to destruction. Therefore, I will discuss where we can go to find security, what biblical principles lead to healing and how to bring hope in strained relationships.

Since reading the two Arbinger Institute books in 2006, I have been teaching these three lessons in many different countries and cultures. The impact of these lessons in every venue has encouraged me to put them into writing. My wife and I praise God for the changes these principles have brought to our relationships. Now we want to share what we have discovered.

Then God said, "Let us make man in our image, in our likeness, and let them rule over the fish of the sea and the birds of the air, over the livestock, over all the earth, and over all the creatures that move along the ground."

So God created man in his own image, in the image of God he created him; male and female he created them.

God blessed them...

~~ Genesis 1:26-28a

Chapter 1

BUILDING RELATIONSHIPS
Seeing People through God's Eyes

"You really love us, don't you?" That question by a young African pastor startled me as I sat next to him on a log eating corn meal mush. I answered, "Yes I do, but why do you say that?" July 2006 was our fourth trip to Malawi and the second year I had taught at Living Word Bible Institute in Nsaru. The young pastor replied, "You return every year, you sleep in our village and eat our food." Before I could say a word another pastor said, "Most missionaries come to our village, pass out condoms and hurry back to town." What these young men were saying was, "We have a relationship with you."

While teaching church leaders throughout the world we have discovered one important truth – every aspect of life that matters, is based in relationships. My heart beats for Christian leadership; this is what I teach as I travel (that is why many illustrations in these lessons refer to leaders). I believe true leadership is founded on godly relationships. Some leaders have secured a following through manipulation, legalism and/or intimidation. Some purposely plan to control their people by keeping them ignorant and dependent. However, this is not true leadership. God never condones any form of leadership that controls and/or uses people for the leader's advantage. God bases leadership solely upon relationships that bless people.

If I hope to enjoy my Christian experience, I must learn how to build relationships. This will require me learning to see people through the eyes of God – who has built relationships from the Garden to the present.

An *ah ha* moment occurred while Peggy (my wife) and I were sitting in a hotel restaurant in downtown Nairobi, Kenya. It was one of those times when suddenly what you have read, heard and observed seem to converge into realization. That experience sparked the writing of this lesson.

We were seated at a table that touched a windowed wall overlooking the front sidewalk. Outside, a river of people flowed between two nearby bus terminals. We commented on different people we noticed in the crowd. Families were coming and going for visits to relatives in home villages. Businessmen rushed between appointments. Parents tried to keep their children nearby as hawkers and beggars worked the street to make enough to subside one more day. As I watched I remembered an article I had read which warned people traveling in foreign countries of the temptation to see people merely as *part of the landscape*.

As I reflected on the article, I recalled the pre-field orientation that Peggy and I attended for our first short-term mission team. The preparation was guided by a former missionary who warned us to resist seeing people as cast members in a drama.

> "These people don't change costumes and go home when their act is complete. The people you see on the streets and in the villages are *real people* – they were there yesterday, they will be there tomorrow and will most likely be there every day doing the same tasks for years to come."

As I watched from our table these words suddenly became real. The people we saw before us were neither animated objects nor actors walking by our window; they were living, breathing souls. I turned to Peggy and said, "Do you realize that every one of these people has a story? We could stop any one of them and learn that they have a name and there are people they love and people who love them. Each one has a history unique only to them."

At that moment it hit me how God sees each of us as individuals. We are not a flow of objects on the face of the earth. He knows our name and our story. He cares and He has shown that He does. At that point I made a renewed commitment to attempt to do the same wherever I serve. Relationships that make a difference grow out of our willingness to see people as God sees them.

I experience difficulty with this. I struggle with seeing people as people rather than *objects*.[2] If I do not remind myself, my mind becomes numb to individuals and their stories. I tend to see life as my personal drama. Everything focuses on my hopes, needs, cares and fear. The cast (people I encounter daily) has a responsibility to be aware of these and to make my role successful. If I do not remind myself of Paul's admonition to see others as important (Ro 12:3), I begin to inflate my personal significance by seeing people for how they affect my life. When I do this, I miss out on the richness of relationships.

Surely we all seek successful relationships, whether in missions, church, business, education or family. *Relationships* are an indispensable key to each area of life. Regardless of the culture, heritage, knowledge, degrees and titles bring little satisfaction if not accompanied by proper relationships. And *relationships* only happen when I begin to see people as special, unique individuals just as God sees them. Every person I meet is created in the image of God and has a name and a story.

When I experience times of difficulty in relationships I have discovered I can rejuvenate the connection by readjusting my eyes. I have to guard against dehumanizing, not only the people passing by, but members of my family and those within my sphere of influence. It takes concentration to see others through God's eyes. Therefore, let me share three wonderful ways in which God sees each of us and encourage you to take a new look at each person who touches your life.

1. God Sees Us as Worthy of Relationship

Worthy of a Relationship that Brings Blessing

I had a scriptural epiphany several years ago while studying scripture in an effort to clearly understand God's purpose in history. As I traced God's plan through His story, I discovered God simply desires *to have a people to bless*.[3] His plan began with Adam and Eve in the Garden of Eden where His love and blessings were poured out on the garden's occupants. When they walked away from a relationship with the Heavenly Father, He chose Abraham's family to bless and make them recipients of His love. When Israel continually broke the covenant, God chose from among the Gentiles "a people for himself" (Acts 15:14). According to the vision seen by the Apostle John, a voice will shout with finality, "Now [at last the plan has reached its climax and] the dwelling of God is with men, and he will live with them. They will be his people, and God himself will be with them and be their God. (Rev 21:3 author's commentary). God will have accomplished His purpose.

God's purpose to have a people to bless contains the astounding fact of *imago dei* – the understanding "the image of God" resides in every person. If we take the Genesis record seriously (Gen 1:27, 5:1-2, Col 3:10), we realize that every individual we see during our daily experience bears in their soul His *likeness* and, therefore, should be treated as such.

As I look at the people who intersect my life, I must ask myself if I see *imago dei* – people God desires to bless. Every person I meet is an individual God loves intensely and for whom Jesus died. This thought has to remain constant whether in peace or during conflict.

Our carnal minds do not make this way of thinking easy. For example, Greek philosophers believed "Woman was created as man's eternal curse ... [A] deadly race ... who live amongst mortal men to their great trouble."[4] American historians write that English and European settlers distrusted and took advantage of the Indians who had lived on the land for generations. Many settlers believed, "The only good Indian [American native] is a dead Indian."[5] I have interviewed modern missionaries who describe their calling as, "taking the gospel to the *heathens/pagans*." In 2004, I led a mission pre-field orientation for a Southern California church. One man said, "I want to go to see if it is true that God loves *those people* as much as He loves us [i.e. Americans]."

In all of these circumstances, there is a disconnect with God's view of people. If I approach people believing myself better than they, wondering if God loves them more than me, it will be difficult to build a relationship that gives me permission to share God's story – let alone the opportunity to speak into their life.

When I was in high school I was moved by the testimony of Stuart Hamblin, a country western entertainer who turned to Christ after years of destructive living. In response to his new-found relationship to God he penned the words to the song, "How Big Is God?"

> Though men may strive to go beyond
> the reach of space
> To crawl beyond the distant shining
> stars
> This world's a room so small within my
> Master's house
> The open sky's but a portion of his
> yard.
>
> How big is God, how big and wide is
> His domain
> To try to tell these lips can only start
> He's big enough to rule his mighty
> universe
> Yet small enough to live within my
> heart.[6]

I am still awestruck when I consider Hamblin's description of our Father. These words remind me of

God's challenge to Job as He revealed His presence among the stars, on the ocean floor and with the mountain goats and eagles (Job 38 and 39). When I think of the magnitude of all God is and what He controls, it is humbling to know that He knows me (Jn 10:3), my days (Ps 139:16) and my needs (Mt 6:8). However, I must always remember that the same is true for my wife, my neighbor, the people with whom I work and the people walking down the street. They are also people God knows, loves and treats as real people.

When I stand amazed at the bigness and power of God and that He sees me, I am not alone. In His eyes I am worthy of a blessed relationship; and He has commissioned me to be an ambassador of this blessed relationship. I must learn to intentionally look at another person and see *imago dei* and say, "This is a person as real as me and with whom God desires a relationship."

In spite of my best efforts, I have caused or experienced strained relationships. In most cases it happens with a person whom I had initially viewed as *worthy* of a relationship. A separation occurred because I lost sight of that person's *worthiness*. I allow my mind to dehumanize them and see them apart from God. "How could God desire a relationship with a person who acts like that?" I do this believing God and I know their error. Rather than setting a course for reconciliation, as God has done for me, I set out to correct them, change them or separate from them. In doing so, I miss out on

God's blessings for my life and the blessing of being reconciled with a person worthy of relationship.

When a friend introduced me to Peggy, it was love at first sight. I knew I wanted to marry her before I knew her name. The more I got to know her the more beauty I saw in her. During our courtship we saw differences in each other, but because of our commitment to each other we refused to believe they would grow into problems. We married two and a half years after our first meeting.

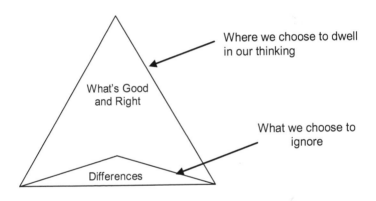

What's Good and Right

Where we choose to dwell in our thinking

What we choose to ignore

Differences

About three months after our wedding I noticed she had some habits and qualities I thought she needed to change. At that point I no longer saw her as the woman whom I was to bless, but a woman in error who needed correction. A recurring battle began and was waged until we learned to accept the beauty of our differences.

Most relationships into which I enter are based on the good qualities I see in the other person. Those good qualities overpower my thinking to the point I do not realize (or am not willing to admit) some idiosyncrasies linger underneath. It not only happens in marriages, it also happens in the hiring practices of the business world, in choosing a team and in searching for a church. We tend to choose our friends, our spouse, and our teammates based on the good we see; we give little attention to any potential problems. We confidently believe the *good* we see will overpower any underlying problems.

This pyramid illustration helps me understand what happens to these good relationships.

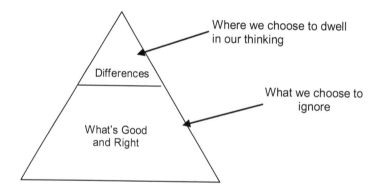

After I have been in a relationship for a period of time, I become more and more aware of the character traits or habits I was so willing to overlook in the beginning. Author Edith Schaeffer claims we will find problems in any person.

"If you find anybody with strong positive traits, you're going to find some strong negative traits, too. Anybody! People are different, and you have to do your best to understand the person . . ."[7]

When I begin to concentrate on what I perceive to be a problem, I allow *differences* to rise to the top. Perceiving them as problems needing correction, I initiate my strategy to change the person and, unwittingly, begin the deterioration of the relationship.

Once I allow *differences* to rise to the top, I spend more time concentrating on them rather than building on *what is right*. I begin to ignore the *good* that first drew me to the relationship. I then decide to set myself against the person or think, "It's my job to change this person." Either decision will result in certain death to a relationship.

God has pronounced a cure for this pyramid problem. When I begin to concentrate on *differences* in a relationship it begins to deteriorate. At those times I must listen as the Holy Spirit prompts me to take my thoughts captive (2 Co 10:5) and begin concentrating on,

> Whatever is true, whatever noble, whatever is right, whatever is pure, whatever is lovely, whatever is admirable – if anything is excellent or

praiseworthy – think about such things ... And the God of peace will be with you.

~~Philippians 4:8-9

Harmony can only be achieved when I learn to accept others as a blessed person and apply God's love to the differences. But, people ask, "What do I do when that 'blessed person' does something to harm our relationship?" We will look at this in greater depth in our next lesson. However, let me suggest the place to begin.

Worthy of a Relationship that Includes Forgiveness

During my first ministry I found myself in a small farming community in Illinois. I was shocked one evening when a deacon stood up during a board meeting and started yelling obscenities because I had failed to announce a youth activity sponsored by the only other church in town and his teenage son had missed it. After his tirade he walked out of the meeting and out of church saying he would never be back as long as I was the minister there. I was stunned and embarrassed.

My first reaction justified my error and said, "Let him walk away. I do not need that kind of person in my life." As I meditated on the situation, God convicted me that this man was His child and worthy of relationship. The next week I reluctantly went to talk to the unhappy farmer but he would not speak to me. I thought, "I have done my part, the next move is up to him." God would not let me get away with that attitude. I needed to ask the farmer to forgive me and be willing to forgive him. My first attempts to bring healing began by greeting him every time I saw him.

Not long after that board meeting, this man was involved in a farming accident. He broke several bones and could only lie in bed. The first time I went to his home he barely talked to me. The more I visited, the more he opened up. I listened to stories about his family who had farmed this land for more than a hundred years. I shared some of my story, and we began to form a new understanding of each other and there was reconciliation.

When the farmer was well enough he returned to church. Two years later, when I submitted my resignation to accept a ministry at another church, this man told me he was sorry I was leaving and asked who I would recommend as my replacement. This reconciliation only took place because God wanted me to see the man through His eyes. This man was as worthy of my forgiveness as I was worthy of God's and the Father wanted to bless us both.

I wish I could say in all my years of ministry every conflict turned out as well as that one.

However, there have been times pride kept me from seeking forgiveness and blinded me to the fact the other person was worthy of my doing what I could to maintain the relationship. Reconciliation happens when I allow God to show me people through His eyes of love and see His desire to bring people under His blessing.

When Adam and Eve broke their covenant with God they lost their place in the Garden. But the story does not end there. God's heart ached, but He did not abandon them. He immediately set a plan for reconciliation. When Israel turned away from God, prophets were sent to draw them back into a relationship. The falling away/reconciliation cycles of the Old Testament clearly picture God's desire for redemption and relationship. This theme carries into the New Testament as Jesus came to bring reconciliation to all who are estranged (2 Co 5:18-19).

Only when I surrender my eyes to God can I see as He sees. My first reaction in conflict tells me to see the other person as a *problem, opponent, enemy* or an *obstacle* in my path. Because of what they have done to me (or someone I love) this person no longer deserves forgiveness.

God disrupts my justifying thoughts by showing me how, even in conflict, God saw Israel as His "treasured possession" (Dt 7:6), the 'apple of His eye" (Zech 2:8). The only title I should bestow on another person, other than *brother* or *sister,* is *fellow struggler.* For this reason Paul admonishes us to "be kind and compassionate to one another, forgiving each other, just as in Christ God forgave you" (Eph 4:32).

There is truth in seeing people as worthy of a blessing whether I am meeting people of a different culture, functioning within my family or participating on a team. God calls me to see each person through His eyes. To do so, I must accept the uniqueness of each individual and see him or her as worthy of relationship and worthy of forgiveness for anything that would block that relationship.

Seeing people worthy of a blessing is only the first truth I have discovered for seeing people the way God sees. The second key sounds easy, but many people find it very difficult and, therefore, dismiss its importance.

2. God Knows My Name

I learned early in my ministry the most important possession a person has (regardless of culture) is *his/her name.* The sweetest sound to the human ear is the sound of one's name. We honor people when we can remember their name. By using a name we let a person know we care enough to know them; it expresses our acceptance of them as a *person.*

Therefore, my next step to demonstrating I believe a person worthy of a relationship requires me to learn his/her name. Jesus described himself as the Good Shepherd and claimed to know each by name (Jn 10:3). When God spoke to Moses he assured him he knew his name (Ex 33:12, 17) and revealed His own name to Moses. When God directed the Levites to take a census of Israel, He directed each person be listed *by name* (Num 1:2). Jesus surprised numerous people by calling them by their name (e.g. Zacchaeus – Lk 19:5).

It was during my first months as a young pastor I learned the impact of someone knowing my name. A mutual friend introduced me to the late Dr. Doug Dickey, who led a campus ministry at Purdue University at the time. He had written a popular book about campus ministries and was in great demand as a speaker. My initial introduction to Dr. Dickey lasted about two minutes. However, three months later I met him for the second time. I was shocked when he called me by name. A relationship was born and I later asked him how he had remembered my name. He shared with me that when he was a young man in the ministry he learned the importance of names and God granted his prayer for the gift to remember names. Before that day I had used the excuse, "I'm not very good with names." I needed to get past that self-justification and that day I, too, prayed for the ability to remember names.

Our experience has proven that the importance of names transcends cultures. I had an interesting conversation about names with a Malawi woman. I was wearing a tee shirt that showed a large bar code across the front, with the words, "Not just another [number]." The woman asked me what the picture meant. I tried to explain that lines represented numbers which a computer can read. In our conversation I told her the shirt means we tend to no longer see people as people; we reduce them to numbers. I went on to say, "According the United States government," I am not 'Robert D. Kuest; I am '555-55-5555' (a government-given number)." The woman's response startled me, "We don't use numbers, but we don't always see people." I was reminded that it does not take a computer to dehumanize people.

Peggy and I have experimented with how people respond when they hear their name. When we enter a restaurant or store we try to notice the server's name and address them by name. We are amazed how people's countenance changes when they are seen as a person, and not "your servant." Sometimes we get a glimpse of their personal story. In one case our restaurant server did not have a name badge. So, I asked her, "May we know the name of the person serving us?" She brightened up and told us. She returned often to our table and during the course of our meal we learned about her schooling and her plans after she completed her course work.

However, I must share a mistake I made when this need to know names taught me a lesson in cultural sensitivity. I was teaching at a small African Bible college and asked my students to stand before the class and share a bit of their life story. Of the thirteen men who shared, only one mentioned his wife by name. The others had simply said, "My wife" or "The Mother of (using the name of their oldest child). When they referred to other women they said, "The Wife of . . ." I made a comment about this and challenged them to learn and use the women's names. Later a man whom I respect took me aside and explained that in their culture the highest distinction a person can give a woman is to refer to her as *married* and/or a *mother*. Therefore, to call her "The Wife of . . ." or "The Mother of . . ." tells the village that she is a fulfilled woman. Therefore, my challenge was not to learn the names of the women, but the names of her husband or oldest child. The principle remains the same.

While not all cultures use proper names, all cultures have a way of addressing a person as acceptable and unique. Whether it is a proper name or an honored distinction, by using a *name* we bring a person out of anonymity to personhood. We must remember God knows our name; therefore, we cannot lose the importance of a name.

Twentieth Century Fox's 2007 production, *Amazing Grace,* tells the story of William

Wilberforce, the man credited with ending the slave trade in England. I was stricken by a scene reenacting a conversation with John Newton, his former pastor who, prior to his conversion, was the captain of a slave ship. Throughout the movie Newton speaks of his *twenty thousand ghosts* (the number of Africans he brought on his ships). In the scene, the elderly Newton says, "My twenty thousand ghosts, they all had names – beautiful African names. We called them with grunts, noises. We were just apes, they were humans." His words struck me; I must also come to that realization if I am going to lead people to the throne of God.

I am a person; I have a name. I am not a number; I have a name that even God knows. Each person has a name that makes he or she special. When I neglect a person's name, I neglect a part of what makes him or her unique. If I desire to see people the way God sees people, I need to let people know their name is important to me.

3. God Knows My Story

Knowing God wants to bless people and learning their name are only the first two steps in my journey to seeing people through His eyes. If I want to build lasting relationships I must continue to keep my eyes and ears open and experience the beauty of this third step. Here we truly begin to connect with another person and deepen our relationship.

Peggy and I have a unique privilege every May to participate in a week of training for college students preparing for summer missionary work. Among our goals for the week is helping them learn to work in harmony and purpose. Three of the most critical exercises of the week are to prepare students to share their story. The first night of the retreat they use pictures and words from old magazines to create a collage picturing what is important in their life. In the second session, closed to all but those with whom they will be directly involved during the summer, they share the heart, hurts and joys of their story. During the third "story session" we coach each student in how to briefly tell their story to an international audience. By sharing their life journeys, students who arrived as strangers are transformed into colleagues. Relationships grow stronger, and those bonds will help each person through the stresses of the summer.

I enjoy visualizing God walking in the Garden with Adam and Eve, fellowshipping with them so they would know Him and feel His desire to know them. David says God helps to write our story while in our mother's womb (Ps 139:13, 16). God is vitally concerned about who we are, where we are and what we are experiencing. He does not abandon us following creation. David, in fact, suggests we can find no place on Earth where we can get away from God knowing us (Ps 139:7-10). We are that important to Him.

God's vigilance far surpasses my own. I have a tendency to concentrate so much on my own story that I fail to take an interest in another's story. I need to make an effort to see people through God's eyes. I can become so busy I only see moving bodies that hold very little meaning. Because of this, I can preach, teach or lead a meeting and only see faces blurred by lack of personal knowledge.

Let me illustrate what I mean. If I showed you a picture of my grandchildren you would very politely make comments about how good looking they are (I am positive this would be your response). For most of you, the picture would hold little meaning and would soon be forgotten. However, if you knew our granddaughter's story, (she had three open-heart surgeries before she was five years old), you would ask, "Which one is she? How is she doing now?" The picture would take on a whole new meaning to you because you knew just one story. (By the way – We praise God for our granddaughter's good health!)

Just the positive mention of a person's story can brighten a relationship. While checking luggage for an overseas flight, a ticket agent noticed my birth date in my passport. He said, "Happy Birthday two days ago, Mr. Kuest. I hope you had a good one." My spirits immediately lifted. I no longer saw myself as one of hundreds waiting in a long queue; I felt like a real person. The same response comes when I greet someone and mention or ask a question about their story. It shows we care enough to remember or notice.

The reverse is also true. In one popular U.S. restaurant the server writes his/her name on the paper table covering. During one visit I picked up the pen and wrote Peggy's and my name under his. Never once during our visit did he call us by name or ask us anything about "our story" ("Where are you from?" "What brings you to this place?" "Are you dining out for a special occasion?") The more he ignored our name (even though we used his name), the more I felt unimportant to him. We were just a table in his assigned area. Perhaps my expectations were too high, but I left with a negative feeling. It is possible in my busyness to become blind to people, only noticing before me faceless objects that make my job possible.

When I walk into an African village I want to remember that the people I see are special *individuals*, each with their own story. The woman with a baby tied to her back as she beats the maize in her home-made mill has a story unique to her. The toothless old man sitting in front of his hut used to be an energetic child running through the village. He has known joys and heartaches as he married and raised a family.

There is a story behind why the man in Myanmar chose to become a Buddhist monk. Real life events led the young woman in Thailand to stand on the street corner offering her body to anyone who will pay her price. The broken person entering the church door did not experience their life collapse in one night. My crusty next-door neighbor, my estranged relative, they all have a story. By wanting to hear their story I show them value. By knowing their story I can be a better friend and/or a better leader. By listening, I earn the right to speak. By caring, I begin to see people the way God sees people.

When I was leading a church it was important for me to know the people to whom I was preaching. As I prepared to preach I would often write two or three names at the top of my study notes, names of people I would hope my message would help. Two or three times during a year I would go into the empty auditorium, sit next to the pulpit and envision the people who would normally occupy certain seats (all around the world people are creatures of seating habits). I would stare at their seat and remind myself of the chapter currently being written in their life story. The chairs tells stories of one person who battles a disease, another who tries to restore a broken relationship, a single mother who faces the challenges of raising her children, a man who just lost his job and a new believer who just discovered the joys of walking with Christ. As I rehearsed each story in my mind it would help me to focus my ministry on real people with real needs.

Author Burt Goldman writes about understanding a person's needs:

> To understand what a relationship is, how to bring one about, how to enhance one, and why relationships are diminished and lost, one must understand the power of a person's needs.
>
> The most important things in the world, to us, are the things we believe that we need. Needs affect opinions, attitudes, and viewpoints. Generally we're more aware of unfulfilled needs than the ones that are consistently met.[8]

The goal to see real people faces a dangerous roadblock. My ego rises desiring to become so involved in my own story I fail to accept that others have one too. I can justify the way I think and act by the events that wrote my personal story – "My parents treated me this way." "My traditions and beliefs must be accepted." I can demand that others understand and accept me but never make an attempt to accept them. I have a tendency to ignore the fact other people also have a heritage that affects the way they think and act.

There is a constant temptation to ignore another's story and begin to see them as an obstacle to my effectiveness. I refuse to admit they act and make decisions based on their own script. Therefore, I set a goal to change them so they will reason and handle situations the way I do. The quickest way to destroy a marriage or a team is for me, or any other member, to set out to change the others. When this becomes my focus, I will wake up one day and look at my wife and/or team members and wonder what happened to our relationship. This all happened because I usurped God's responsibility to bring needed changes.

I admit, however, not everyone stands in line to tell me their story. An unconscious fear causes some people to believe, "If you knew the real me, you would not like me." In his book, Why Am I Afraid To Tell You Who I Am?,[9] John Powell answers his title-question by saying, "I am afraid to tell you who I am, because, if I tell you who I am, you may not like who I am, and it's all that I have." Many people do not like their stories. They might find it easy to tell their name and a few surface facts about their life. Nevertheless, they hold the heart of their story back until they know they can trust us with it. My responsibility as a leader, team member, neighbor or family member challenges me to build that trust and show the same interest in each person's story as God shows in mine.

Finding joy in our Christian walk depends on this third key to relationships. God knows my story. He knows my needs, even before I pray them (Mat 6:8). God, in His wisdom, uses His position and power to meet my needs and bring change. I am not an obstacle to Him; I am not a face in the crowd. Neither should I, as a leader or family man, allow those in my care to become merely faces. The more I know their story, the stronger the relationship. This sets us up for the final key to seeing people through God's eyes.

4. God Knows My Potential

My heart resonates with this final step. When I was in elementary and secondary school, teachers and counselors saw me as a child with little or no potential. Twice during my last year of high school my guidance counselor called me to his office to talk me out of attending a university. He told me, "You'll never make it. Why don't you try vocational training?" However, my family and my pastor were giving me a different message. They believed in me and encouraged me to follow my dream. With their encouragement I pursued a university education. Today I have three earned degrees, including a doctorate.

I will never forget the day Peggy and I accompanied three African pastors to the office of their American leader. They wanted us to meet him because he was responsible for teaching leadership. As we talked, the American said, "I plant the churches, I train the leaders and when I see that the church has stability I turn it over to a national." He finished by saying, "We do not count anything a national does because it will not last." I did not understand the man so later when we arrived at his house I asked the African pastor, "Did I hear what I thought I heard?" He said, "Yes, you heard him and we have heard him say it before." In that same year that denomination survived a near split over the issue of the nationals' competence to be in leadership. What a misunderstanding of God's view of people.

Allow me to ask you a question. "What do Moses, Gideon, David, Jeremiah, Amos and Peter have in common?" They were all men whom the world would not have chosen for leadership. Moses had a long list of reasons why Pharaoh would never listen to him (Ex 3-4). Gideon could not see himself as a leader because, "My clan is the weakest in Manasseh, and I am the least in my family" (Jdg 6:15). David's father never considered his youngest son as a prospect for God's anointing (1 Sa 16:11-12). Jeremiah thought his young age disqualified him (Jer 1:6). Amos was "neither a prophet nor a prophet's son" (Am 7:14). As a fisherman Peter most likely lacked any formal education, but Jesus saw his ability (Jn 1:42). In spite of these *disadvantages*, God used these men to proclaim His message.

No matter where in the world we teach, *burnout* emerges as a major problem among leaders. A major contributor to this is the failure of leaders to see potential in their people. Church leaders all over the world report being tired. They relate how they must preach, teach, organize the youth program, plan and lead the worship service, etc. I get tired just listening to them. I ask, "Don't you have anyone to help you?" Typically they respond, "No one in my congregation can do this work." To which I ask, "Who are you training?" I have had pastors tell me, "I have no one in my congregation I can train." This thinking robs us of one of the greatest joys of our Christian walk, seeing people grow and serve in the Kingdom.

To experience this joy, I must see people the way God sees them. From the very beginning God empowered people with potential. In the Garden He put His spirit in Adam so that he could take responsibility for animals, birds and fish (Ge 1:26). He trusted Noah, Abraham, Moses, David, and the list goes on. Jesus called twelve men, trained them and left the work to them to continue. We never find the Apostle Paul without a person in training. He told the Romans and the Corinthians that God had given special gifts to every believer for the purpose of ministry. He specifically told Timothy to train others who would train others (2 Ti 2:2). He instructed the Ephesian leaders "to prepare God's people for works of service" (Eph 4:12); a principle he never would have given had he not believed people had the potential to serve. God does see us with potential that can be developed into competency. That is why people lead ministries and not angels.

Peggy and I see similar problems in marriages where one spouse treats the other as if they have no abilities. We have seen both men and women guilty of this thinking. We know of husbands who come home from work and want a full accounting of his wife's day – which he planned out for her. He tells her how to clean the house, how to raise the kids, how to cook and how to make him happy. His wife exists as an object brought into the house to support his role as a man. We have also seen wives who have treated their husbands like incompetent idiots. She only stays with him because she needs a legitimate father for the children she wants in her story. These spouses pass their attitudes on to their children who begin to speak in the same way. Both spouses treat their partner as an object, not a person.

I heard a well-known pastor demonstrate another aspect of this "potential thinking" when he gave his closing remarks at a conference. "I am leaving after this session," he said, "because I have to go home to line up people for the nursery, check on the worship team and Sunday school teachers so we can have services this weekend. I want to make everything ready before Sunday." This man, and others like him, sees leadership as running a machine. A machine runs with many moving parts; all must be in place and in working order. They do not see people; they see gears, cogs, springs and rotors. They believe their responsibility is to plug people into roles so the machine works. Leaders remove broken parts and replace them with new. Toss the damaged away; one cannot concern themselves with relationship or caring. Leaders who see people as expendable parts to their well-run machine do not bother to know stories or even notice abilities. They search only for live bodies to fill vacancies.

As a husband I must fight off this same thinking. I cannot allow myself to lose touch with my wife's personhood by seeing her as my personal cook, laundry woman, house cleaner, sex partner and mother or nursemaid to my children. Some women fail to see their husband as a person by beginning to look at their man as a pay check, a security blanket and man to give them children. The litany of misery or multiple marriages tells a history. They have forgotten, or never learned to look at each other through the eyes of God, who has given every person potential and willingly recognizes it in each of us.

I have a theory which will never be proven. I believe the fastest runner in the world has never been found. He/she lives in a village or town far off the main road where no one has ever discovered their potential. I believe some of the strongest church leaders have never been developed for God's purposes because no one saw their potential. All around us God has placed people with huge potential. As a leader my responsibility demands that I find them and help them grow. However, in order to accomplish this, I must first develop a relationship of trust that gives me permission to lead.

Conclusion

I contrast the difference between seeing people as objects or seeing people as God sees them by comparing the eyes of Jesus to the eyes of other religious leaders. A Pharisee arose every morning and had a list of seven *objects* that he thanked God he was *not like*. "Thank God," he would pray, "I am not a Samaritan, a Gentile, a woman, a child, poor, sick or lame." During his righteous routes throughout the day he did all he could to avoid these objects so they would not tarnish his purity. But yet he considered himself a leader of the people.

Jesus, on the other hand, saw people wherever he went. He touched and blessed people others would ignore, he called people by name, he recognized a story in process and he acknowledged potential. He blessed children, ministered to Samaritans, Gentiles and women. He recognized the sacrifices of the poor; He healed the lame and restored the blind. He knew each person carried the image of His Father.

When Jesus came into the city of Nain (Lk 7:11-16) there was a funeral in progress. Any Pharisees present would have avoided the scene because they would have seen a poor widow (woman) and a dead body. Jesus saw a hurting woman who had lost a beloved son. Where Pharisees walked away from these disgusting objects of life, Jesus approached and used his power and position to meet her need.

No one knows us better than God. No one loves us more than our Lord. No one believes in us more than our Heavenly Father. He saw us when we were living a hopeless life (Eph 2:12). By His good pleasure He adopted us as His children (Eph 1:5). We became His chosen people (1 Pt 2:9), His treasured possessions (Dt 7:6) and His children (1 Jn 3:1).

This is how God sees me, how I need to see myself and each person I encounter in life. I need to see each person as worthy of a blessing, to know their name and their story. I want a relationship that earns the right to encourage potential. I desire the ability to love others as I love myself because I accept that I am important to God – so is my spouse, my neighbor, my fellow worker, and the person across the room from me. Wherever I see people, I want to see them as God sees them. This is what brings joy to our Christian experience.

Discussion Questions
Chapter One

1. Assignments for next session:

   A. As you go about your daily contacts (family, neighborhood, work, sports, etc) make a conscious effort to think *Imago Dei* ("This is a person created in the image of God"). Note if it makes any difference in your attitude toward them.

   B. Sit in a location where there are many people. As people pass you, think, "These are real people whom God loves intensely; each has a name and story unique to them." Be ready to share your experience in the next session.

2. How important is it to you that someone knows your name? Do you get upset when it is mispronounced?

3. Share a time when knowing someone's story made a difference in your relationship with them.

4. As a relationship becomes more familiar, why is it so easy to concentrate on *differences* rather than rejoicing in what is *good*? Discuss the meaning of Philippians 4:8.

Finally, be strong in the Lord and in his mighty power. Put on the full armor of God so that you can take your stand against the devil's schemes. For our struggle is not against flesh and blood, but against the rulers, against the authorities, against the powers of this dark world and against the spiritual forces of evil in the heavenly realms. Therefore put on the full armor of God, so that when the day of evil comes, you may be able to stand your ground, and after you have done everything, to stand.

~~ Ephesians 6:10 - 13

Chapter 2

PROTECTING RELATIONSHIPS

If relationships are the most important ingredient to finding joy in my Christian life, what do I do when someone threatens those bonds? Before I can answer that question I must first understand what pressures these relationships face and what defenses I tend to use when I perceive that my relationships are being threatened.

I have seen pictures of knights riding to war carrying two shields. A long shield attached to their saddle was designed to protect his full body. A second, smaller shield provided mobility in battle. When the knight arrived at a battle he had to make a decision about which shield to choose. His choice would determine his ability to function in the midst of battle.

I also carry two shields. Daily, sometimes hourly, I face the knight's choice – "Which shield will I use when I perceive a threat to an important relationship?" My choice will determine the health of my relationships, as well as my ability to function in God's Kingdom. I want to talk about these two shields, but first let me review the purpose of carrying a shield.

Immediately, I think a shield exists to prevent injury or death. However, according to my observations, we face two totally different ways of dying and one comes much easier than the other.

1. Two Deaths

Physical Death

As a warrior the obvious purpose of my shield is to protect my life, to deflect weapons that threaten injury or death. This point is so obvious and well known I do not need to spend time here. Like most people, I will do whatever necessary to prevent harm to my body. However, *physical death* does not rank as the worst death I could experience, nor is it the one from which I feel the strongest need to protect myself.

Relational Death

A young woman came to my office for counsel concerning a painful relationship. After explaining her situation she said, "I would rather die than lose this relationship." She was not exaggerating and I have heard her words expressed by many others in various ways. In fact, even though we don't say it aloud, most of us would agree..

Relational death is a far greater threat to my being than the loss of life. God created us for relationships (1 Co 1:9, 2 Co 13:14, Php 2:1, 1 Jn

1:3-7). Therefore, the need for acceptance as a significant individual resides deep within my soul.

I function at my best when I sense a healthy relationship. God created us as both spiritual and social beings. One Christian psychologist claims "rejection is the greatest fear that a person faces."[10] This fear becomes the driving force behind all my decisions. Andrew Olson, a psychologist working with New Mission Systems International, refers to this as a "fear of death" (death to a relationship). He claims that people base all decisions on the perception of what will allow a person to live (relationally), even if it means the death (physical or relational) of others. When I sense danger within a conversation or in actions I perceive to threaten my acceptance in relationships, I have a tendency to think, "I will not die as a result of this interaction."

In order to prevent my death to my acceptability in relationships, I have a choice between the two shields I carry for protection. Let's take a look at these shields and why I believe I need to raise one of them.

2. Two Shields

The Shield of Deception

Purpose of the Shield of Deception – To Protect my Acceptability

I have devised a defense plan to protect my ability to be in relationships. I have the availability of a shield behind which I can stand to protect myself from verbal weapons hurled by other people. Those words, like a sword wielded by a warrior, hit my *shield* and deflect toward another person; thus passing the blame to that person. ("I'm not the one who is going to die in this situation; he or she is.") The problem is, however, this shield prevents me from seeing the truth of my words and actions. It convinces me I have no part in the problem and someone else must take the blame. It also convinces me I am on my own because "God cannot or will not help me in this situation." In other words, "I am deceived."

The shield protects my body and mind; however, I also have a weapon at my disposal – The sword of Blame. A good warrior must not only protect himself, he must be able to fight. Believing this, we raise our sword and point to the real problem (more on this later). Therefore, with shield in one hand and sword in the other, I equip myself for self-protection. Or so I think.

Why I Raise the Shield of Deception

The following diagram and explanation describes a five-part mental process my mind uses to quickly evaluate every conversation or report. It determines if those words and/or actions support my relational survival or threaten it. My reactions to words and/or actions are motivated by my perception of how they will affect my ability to be seen as a *worthwhile* person in the eyes of those with whom I desire a relationship.

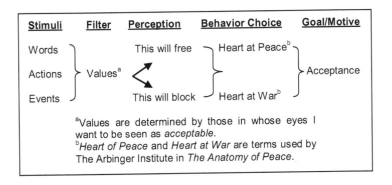

Stimuli	Filter	Perception	Behavior Choice	Goal/Motive
Words		This will free	Heart at Peace[b]	
Actions	Values[a]			Acceptance
Events		This will block	Heart at War[b]	

[a]Values are determined by those in whose eyes I want to be seen as *acceptable*.
[b]*Heart of Peace* and *Heart at War* are terms used by The Arbinger Institute in *The Anatomy of Peace*.

A. Goal/Motive

I must begin with the end (the right side of the chart), the goals or motives for my words and actions. Everything that happens in the transaction (chart process) focuses on my achieving acceptability. Every behavior choice has this goal. Robert McGee claims our goal is *significance,* to be seen as acceptable and appreciated by those we value.[11] Above all else, every action or word I choose has the goal of me being accepted as a person worthy of *relationships*.

B. Stimuli

I remember standing in a university office waiting for my wife to get off work when a professor walked by and said, "Who told you that was a good looking tie?" A few days later I was back to pick up my wife when the same professor walked by and said, "You realize, don't you, your Doctor of Ministry degree is not an academic degree?" It had been years since I had had any contact with this man. Prior to these two events I had not said or done anything I could remember as offensive. However, I was faced with the necessity of responding to these remarks.

Each and every day I must process words and events in my life over which I have no control; yet, I find myself forced to choose a response to them. I have no control over the words someone speaks to me or about me. I did not put the words in their mouth. Good or bad, I must respond verbally, physically or silently.

I not only face words, but at times I must respond to a person's actions. I once saw a man extend his hand in greeting and the other person slapped him. The man did not make that person strike, but he did have to choose a response to the blow. I have no control over accidents, diseases, and other stimuli, but they force me to choose which shield I will raise in defense. However, the next step in my thinking process helps with my selection for protection.

C. Filter

Over the years I have developed a value system through which I filter every word or action. My brain constantly processes every stimulus, deciding whether it frees or blocks my acceptability. As I process the information through the filter (my value system) I decide on a defense to protect my being seen as a person of significance.

Like the Apostle Paul, I also have two natures that war within me (Ro 7:14-24). These natures make up the basis of my filtering system. I liken them to having a filtering system that has two channels. I have to decide through which opening I will allow the stimulus to be processed. I have a very self-centered and demanding *fleshly nature*. However, I also have the option of my *spiritual nature* which seeks Christlikeness. My reaction to the outward stimuli will depend on which of these natures I use to process the input.

The fleshly channel of my filter includes values written by the person or people to whom I desire to see me as *acceptable*. If I want you to see me as acceptable, I will attempt to evaluate what you expect in a relationship. If I want God to see me as acceptable, then scripture writes my values. If I want to be acceptable to a youth gang, that gang will write my values. I will process each stimulus according to my evaluation as to whether or not that event will present me as acceptable to my chosen audience. Perhaps, for this reason Paul warns, "Bad company corrupts good character" (1 Co 15:33).

D. Perception

I am an expert on me. Robert McGee writes that, in relationships, "each person themselves is the only expert on self."[12] Therefore, my values filter holds truth for me. As the stimuli pass through my filter, whether fleshly or spiritual, I make a judgment of whether this event will free or promote acceptability to my chosen audience.

If, as I process words and actions, I perceive one has the potential to block my acceptability, then I will chose a reaction I believe will clear my way to that goal. If necessary, I will raise the Sword of Blame to show the true problem. For this reason teenage years in most cultures are seen as *battle years.* The teen wants to be seen as acceptable to his/her peers while also feeling a pull toward independence. The parents set rules to guide the child to maturity (which, if successful, will promote the parents' acceptability before their peers). However, the child identifies those rules as the parent blocking their goal of peer-acceptability and, therefore, chooses a countering behavior. If parents have not built a relationship of trust this can lead to all out war.

E. Behavior Choice

"Behaviors are tools used to get some result or confirm my sense of self-worth. These tools are also used to ward off things I do not want."[13] When I perceive an unwanted stimulus attacking my acceptability I use a *shield* to protect it and the sword to attack my perception of the true source. The Arbinger Institute says this choice sets my heart at war or at peace.[14]

Raising the Shield of Deception – Choosing War

Visualize with me. A village man enters his house in the evening and his wife asks, "Did you finish planting the field today?" He suddenly explodes, "I am a busy man. I have many chores and responsibilities. What makes you think I could get the field done today?" Then he asks, "Why are you worried about me; what about you? I saw you drinking tea with the neighbor. And, now my dinner is going to be late." She reacts, "I raise your kids, I do your laundry, I fix your food and all you care about is whether or not dinner is on time. You never care about me."

What happened in this scene? The man perceived the woman's question as an accusation of laziness. Such an evaluation blocks his hopes of being seen amongst his peers as a successful farmer. Perhaps he thinks, "I cannot allow her question to prove her mother right about me."

43

Therefore, he set his heart at war and raised his Shield of Deception to protect himself. Then, he raised his sword and pointed blame at her – believing that he deflected the threatening conversation away from himself. "I am not going to die in this exchange, she is." She reacts in a similar manner, grabs her shield and sword and now they are at war.

I can also raise my Shield of Deception if I perceive someone has negative feelings about me. I approach that person thinking he or she does not like me or I am not qualified to be in their presence. In such times I have to fight to keep my defenses down. There is no need to feel *war* where none exists. Neither should I choose *war* even if negative vibrations come from the other person.

I feel the need for self-preservation because of my fear of relational death. My fleshly nature screams, "I will not die here!" However, a second deception causes my heart to choose war. It comes when I am tempted to believe "God cannot/will not help me in this situation." Therefore, I feel I am on my own; I'm the only one who can save me."

Conflicts are "ultimately a choice of whether to follow or reject God's sovereignty."[15] To justify raising this shield I must convince myself and others "I am right. I am not the problem; the blame belongs somewhere else. I am not going to die here. This person blocked my goal and there is nothing in scripture or through the leading of God's Holy Spirit that is going to help me; I must be the one to act."

I had one unforgettable day of counseling while ministering to a church in Arizona. Three people had asked to see me and I scheduled them throughout one day. After listening to each woman explain the troubles caused by their husband, I said, "Let me share with you what scriptures says about your situation." The first woman immediately looked at her watch and said, "Oh no, I forgot I have an appointment; I must go." She got up and walked out of my office. The second woman responded by saying, "God does not understand my situation." The third said, "Scripture doesn't speak to modern problems, it cannot help me." All three people left my office convinced they must keep their shields raised and swords raised. All three ended their marriages in all out war and divorce. This perhaps speaks to my success as a counselor, but it also explains the deception that says, "God cannot/will not help me, I must act."

Moses narrates the first historical occurrence of the Shield of Deception and Sword of Blame in the third chapter of Genesis. When God created Adam and Eve He made a covenant with them. In the agreement He warned them if they broke the covenant, "You will surely die" (Ge 2:17). Satan entered the garden disguised as a serpent and pointed his Sword of Blame at God and deceived Adam and Eve into believing, "You will not surely die" (Ge 3:4). He played on their *selfishness* – "I want, God can't/won't." To rephrase the serpent's temptation, "Don't ask what God wants for you; think about you getting what you want." In other words, "God is your problem!"

After choosing to break God's covenant, Adam and Eve ate of the fruit. Suddenly they became aware of their nakedness and God's presence in the Garden. Upon hearing His voice Adam and Eve recognized their sin (Ge 3:7). They also recognized God's awesome presence (Ge 3:8), "He said He would kill us and I know He is capable of doing it." Adam and Eve knew they were in trouble (Ge 3:8-10). Therefore, they hid (Ge 3:8, 10).

God called out, "Adam, where are you?" Knowing what he had done was wrong and believing God could not or would not help him if he spoke the truth, Adam raised his Shield of Deception and deflected the blame back to God, "This is your fault; you gave me this woman. Everything was good here in the garden when it was just you and me. You created this woman and she caused this to happen." Adam then points his Sword of Blame at Eve; "I'm not the problem, she is. If anyone deserves to die here, it is her."

Eve immediately raised her Shield of Deception and aimed her Sword of Blame to deflect the accusation toward the serpent; "I'm not the problem, the serpent is. If anyone is going to die, kill him."

Hiding and blaming have become our response to any situation where we perceive death to our acceptability. Adam and Eve's bush has been replaced by our mental shields.

Strengthening my Shield of Deception – Self-Justification

> The problem is precisely we *can't see [or accept] how we are the problem*. Having the problem we have, nothing we can think of will be a solution ... Self-deception is like this. It blinds us to the true cause of problems, and once blind, all the *solutions* we can think of will actually make matters worse.[16]

Joan had one of the strongest Shields of Deception I encountered as a pastor. She would come to me periodically for counsel; however, I was never convinced she truly sought help. Rather, in my opinion, Joan only wanted to strengthen her justification. During every session she spieled a litany of reasons that vindicated her treatment of her husband. She not only gave me the list of wrongs she had mentally filed, she could give me the year, month, day and time of day the infraction was committed.

The longer I have my Shield of Deception raised, the stronger it must become to hold back what threatens my acceptance. The most frequent tool chosen to intensify *deception* is *justification*. Like Joan, I begin to think of all the reasons I am not the problem and why the *other* is the problem. If I can prove they are the problem, then, in my mind, I am justified to raise my shield and sword. My thinking goes like this:

I Am	You Are[17]
Right	Wrong
The victim	The victimizer
Fair	Unfair
Important	Unappreciative
Always	Never
Consistent	Inconsistent
Compassionate	Insensitive
Going to live	Going to die

The more I justify my thinking, the deeper I fall into self-deception. I "betray" myself. My justification makes the situation more and more difficult to handle. Now, more than ever, I cannot allow myself to be seen as the problem.[18]

Where I live I have to split wood for our fireplace. I learned as a youth on the farm that the best way to do this was to place a wedge in a place where the wood was cracked. With two or three well-placed blows with a heavy hammer, the wood splits. Satan uses the same principle to separate our relationships. He finds a small difference, convinces us that we are right and places a wedge into the crack. With every self-justifying thought we drive the wedge deeper. Each swing magnifies my  virtues – "I am the one who is right/good. This is why I cannot be the one who dies here." Another stroke of the hammer enlarges my deception/justification by bringing to mind the value of my position and why it must be accepted. I will look for people to validate my thinking and even search scripture to find support. With this ammunition, I now have evidence to justify blaming the other person and, thus, the relationship is split.

As demonstrated by the Arbinger Institute, my deception becomes a part of me; I end up carrying these self-justifying images with me into new situations.[19] Therefore, I enter new situations with the Shield of Deception *already* raised."[20] I become a war looking for a place to be fought. Anyone or any situation becomes a potential battleground. The Arbinger Institute explains what happens this way:

> "If people act in ways that challenge the claim made by a self-justifying image, we see

them as threats. If they reinforce the claim made by a self-justifying image, we see them as allies. If they fail to matter to a self-justifying image, we see them as unimportant. Whichever way we see them, they're just objects to us."[21]

Raising My Shield – A Show of Power

Behind the Shield of Deception it is all about *me*. "I am the one who needs to be protected." "I am the one who must be acceptable." "God cannot/will not help me in this situation." "I cannot die in this situation." "I must show my power."

Power hinders learning and growth. It polarizes the issue into sides, for and against. Resolution is linked to pride, personality and persuasion. Someone has to win, someone has to lose; someone has to be right, someone has to be wrong. The incentive is to win, not to learn and grow. The conflict takes on a life of its own, driven by self-protection, saving face and defending reputations. Honest disagreements suddenly become personal attacks ... Escalation can occur when two sides are mutually threatened, each by the other. When this happens, every action requires a counter action, further polarizing the sides ... Both sides want conformity to their perspective. Each side sees the others as a threat to achieving [what] they want."[22]

No one is willing to drop their shield and admit, "I am the problem." Therefore, the battle rages on.

One missionary told me, "I don't use power when things get difficult, I just leave. However, leaving is a power play. I have modified the "Slippery Slope"[23] of choices used by the Peacemakers Ministry to show how we can manipulate a situation by choosing to be either *passive* or *aggressive*. (I

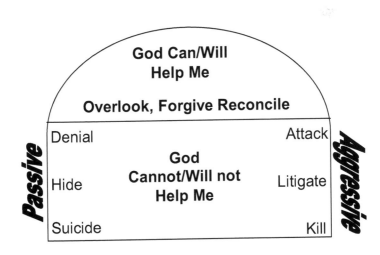

highly recommend Ken Sande's *The Peacemaker*[24] for those who want to go deeper into this subject.)

Passive *Denial* and *Hiding* are just as much of a demonstration of "shield raising" (power) as is an aggressive attack, be it physical or verbal. It attempts to control a situation in a way that does not allow for God's plan. The end result of the passive slide is suicide, either as the ultimate end of the loss of acceptability, or the ultimate act of power.

In order to establish *comfort* behind my Shield of Deception and take the aggressive slide, I have to dehumanize my opposition. My enemy can no longer be seen as *a person*, they must be seen as *an expendable object.* During military training soldiers have this principle engrained in them – "that is not a person you are aiming at, it's the enemy. Do not think of them as a person with a family, with hopes, needs, cares and fears. To do so will lessen your ability to kill." To enforce this, the enemy is given new names. In American military history the Indians became "the redskins," the Japanese became "the japs." The Germans became "krauts." The Arabs are "ragheads." In most conflicts we drop names and the opposition becomes *them, they, those idiots* or some other designation that removes them from personhood.

Doctors taught to give abortions are told not to think of the embryo as a life but to think of it as a piece of flesh. An obstetrician friend told me that this was his medical training. However, when ultra sound was invented and he saw the embryo moving in the mother's womb he realized, "This is a person." From that point on he could no longer perform abortions.

If I recognize my opponent as a person who has a name and a story, a person with "hopes, needs, cares and fears,"[25] I will not be able to point my Sword of Blame at him or her. However, if I consider opponents as less significant than me, I can easily declare them worthy of blame; they can die in those situations. Perhaps this is one reason why Paul warns us, "Do not think of yourself more highly than you ought, but rather think of yourself with sober judgment" (Ro 12:3).

The Battle Is Set – Two Hearts at War

I choose *war* when I raise the Shield of Deception and point my sword of Blame. When I do so, the person facing the tip of my sword feels compelled to raise and justify their own Shield of Deception.

I have seen people physically pointing their sword (index finger) at another person. I once observed a public disagreement between a man and woman. He kept pointing his finger at her until she was leaning backwards. Then she raised her sword (finger) attempting to justify herself by pointing out his error. When she did this, he raised his other hand and held it flat towards her (like a shield) and renewed the strength of his sword. He was not going to be proven wrong, especially in the eyes of those watching. She threw up her Shield of Deception and walked away; she was not going to be the one to die here. She was not giving him the satisfaction by admitting she was wrong.

> By blaming, I invite others to [raise their Shield of Deception], and they then blame me for blaming them unjustly. But because, while I'm [behind my shield], I feel justified in blaming them. I feel that *their* blame is unjust and blame them even more.[26]

In fact, "We promote the very problems we complain about."[27] If I complain about your anger, I will provoke you to anger, push your buttons, and then point my Sword of Blame at you and say, "See, that's just what I'm talking about." If your procrastination upsets me, I will tempt you to relax or withhold information so you do not get started. Then, I will point my sword and say, "See, I'm justified!"

Jesus identified our cross-condemning behavior during The Sermon on the Mount. He warned, "Do not judge, or you too will be judged. For in the same way you judge others, you will be judged, and with the measure you use, it will be measured to you" (Mt 7:1-2). The word Jesus uses that the English translates as *judge* can also be interpreted as, "condemn, punish, avenge, conclude or think."[28] Jesus said, if I use words or actions that cause another to want to go to war against me, that person will use the same criteria to justify their war against me. Then I will begin to push that person to perform the same behavior I am condemning in them so I can justify my battle against their behavior; and the cycle goes round and round.

The Arbinger Institute calls this kind of face off collusion.[29] "In their book, *The Anatomy of Peace*, a *collusion* is defined as a conflict where the parties are inviting the very things they are fighting against."[30] The English word *collusion* describes two people who *agree to deceive* or defraud.[31] Instead of solving the problem I psychologically *agree* to raise my Shield of Deception and go to war. Then, the other person *agrees* to raise his/her shield. A cycle of war begins and the battle intensifies with every trip around the "Cycle of Perception." The diagram below, (adapted from The Arbinger Institute's *Collusion* diagram[32]) shows how *perceptions* promote war. The perceptions and responses continue around and around, growing stronger.

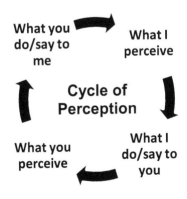

Either party in the conflict can stop the cycle at any time they choose. All I need to do is drop my shield and admit I am the problem and seek reconciliation (more on that in the next lesson).

In a last attempt to justify my deception I ask, "What if the other person is the problem?" There are times in which I have been blindsided by an accusation for which I saw no reason. However, in response I have learned I must answer these questions, "Does my blame (spear pointing) help the other person get better?" "Do my words and actions help me and the other person lower shields and swords?" "Am I promoting war or seeking peace?" War only continues when I give it reason.

Notice the words of David:

> Come and see the works of LORD,
> > The desolations he has brought on the earth.
> He **makes wars cease**
> > to the ends of the earth.
> He breaks the bow and **shatters the spear**;
> > He **burns the shields** with fire.
> Be still, and know that I am God:
> > I will be exalted among the nations,
> > I will be exalted in the earth.

> ~~Psalm 46:8-10
> (emphasis added)

If God is able to cause wars to cease; if He is willing to shatter spears (swords]; if God is able to burn shields, why do our hearts remain at war? Why do we have Christian marriages in all out war? Why are there churches that resemble a war zone? Perhaps I have not learned how to *be still.* Because I continue believing God cannot and will not handle my situation. As a result, I hide behind the wrong shield.

3. God as My Shield
2 Samuel 22:1-4

I have found an invincible protection for my acceptability. In all my struggles to be worthwhile I found a place of peace where I am already loved, but in striving to prove my own significance I did not recognize it. I discovered my shield is only as good as the material from which it is made. No matter how hard I work trying to expose the faults of others it will never create invincible protection. I learned a great lesson from the life of King David about how to maintain a heart of peace, even in the time of war. I will discuss this further in the next lesson; however, let me give you a glimpse of it now.

David had plenty of reasons to set his heart at war. However, he maintained a heart of peace simply because he knew God as a protector. Twenty-five times the Old Testament refers to God as a *shield*. More than fifty times He is described as a "place of refuge." Countless Christian hymns sung for generations paint the same descriptions. God is the one who promises to make wars to cease. Listen to the words of David near the end of a life that constantly faced criticism and war:

> The LORD is my rock, my fortress and my deliverer; my God is my rock, in whom I take refuge, my shield and the horn [strength] of my salvation. He is my stronghold, my refuge and my savior— from violent men you save me. I call to the LORD, who is worthy of praise, and I am saved from my enemies ... As for God, his way is perfect; the word of the LORD is flawless. He is a shield for all who take refuge in him.

> ~~2 Samuel 22:2-4, 31

I pray God will help me understand how to rest in Him, how to take refuge behind His shield. While I worry about being found *acceptable*, David reports: "You are a shield around me, O LORD; you bestow glory on me and lift up my head" (Ps 3:3). Anyone who has read through the Psalms knows that David struggled with understanding why others did not greet him with the same heart of peace with which he willingly met them. He was the victim of many unscrupulous battles. However, even as he cried out to God for help, his mind usually returned to this truth that set his heart at peace:

> "O house of Israel, trust in the Lord — He is their help and shield. O house of Aaron, trust in the Lord — He is their help and shield. You who fear him, trust in the Lord — He is their help and shield
>
> ~~Psalm 115:9–11

The Apostle Peter confirms my trust in God's protection: "Through faith [we] are shielded by God's power" (1 Pt 1:5).

My life, my *acceptability* can hide in God. He made me, loves me and offers to become *my bodyguard*. When my character is attacked, or for any reason when my heart feels threatened, I need to lower my shield and allow my loving God to become "my fortress, my stronghold and my deliverer, my shield, in whom I take refuge" (Ps 144:2).

The Shield of Faith – To Protect from Deception – Ephesians 6:16

Sometimes I feel like I need something more tangible than "hiding behind God." I call out, "Give me a shield, O Lord." For those of us who want to hold something in front of us, God has provided a shield.

I found my tangible shield in Paul's encouragement to the Ephesian Christians to put on the *armor* of God. Our God provides for our daily protection in spiritual warfare. Each piece of armor has a particular purpose in defending my stand for Christ. It includes *The Shield of Faith* given to *block the flaming arrows of the evil one* (Eph 6:16). Whereas the Shield of Deception blocks the truth the Shield of Faith blocks the deception to allow my heart to be at peace. This happens because I believe God's promises and wait on the Lord who can and will act in my situation. And, His abilities stretch far beyond my own. As the writer of Proverbs testifies, "[God] holds victory in store for the upright. He is a shield to those whose walk is blameless" (Pr 2:7). Allow me to add commentary to this verse by asking, "Whose walk is not seeking to place blame"?

Flaming arrows create a scary picture of what the enemy hurls my way. What is Paul describing? We can best understand Paul's picture when we examine the names scripture gives to our spiritual adversary, the one who wants to deceive us into believing we are *unacceptable*, the one who aspires to separate us from God's blessings.

In the Old Testament our antagonist bears the Hebrew name *Satan*, which describes him as an *Accuser*.[33]

I cannot imagine being covered with manure from head to toe. However, in the Prophet Zechariah's vision of Joshua, the High Priest, standing before the throne of God, this was his condition (Zec 3:1-2). In the vision, Satan was accusing Joshua of all kinds of filthiness. God refused to listen and responded to the charges by asking the angels to wash him and give him new clothes (Zec 3:4). Then the Lord recommissioned Joshua,

> If you will walk in my ways and keep my requirements, then you will govern my house and have charge of my courts, and I will give you a place among these standing here.
>
> ~~Zechariah 3:7

This gives me a picture of how God responds to the constant finger-pointing Satan wages against me every day and night before God's throne (Rev 12:10). In response, Paul confidently asks the rhetorical question, "Who can bring a charge against God's children?" (Ro 8:33). The truth is God will not listen to the accusations brought against me by Satan or anyone else. I can trust in that truth. "The Lord is my strength and my shield; my heart trusts in him, and I am helped" (Ps 28:7).

Satan does not stop with accusing us before God. He will plant allegations in my mind against fellow Christians, family members, neighbors, etc. He will make sure I notice every error in their life and cause me to question their love and/or motivations. However, as God refuses to listen to charges against me, so should I turn a deaf ear to the charges the deceiver brings against others. Paul reminds me that my battle is not against people (Eph 6:12). People are not my problem. The problem resides in the spiritual realm.

My battle, however, continues. If bringing accusations against others does not cause me to break my relationship with them and God, then The Accuser will level his Sword of Blame at my own sense of worthiness. "You are not good enough." "You don't have anything to offer to the Kingdom." "You have sin in your past." "You are not worthy to speak for God." Over and over I have self-defeating thoughts aimed at my heart. It is for this very purpose that God provides for us the Shield of Faith – to deflect such false thinking.

My Accuser has another identity that describes a second type of *flaming arrow* I need to block with the Shield of Faith. He is The *Deceiver* – the New Testament description of my enemy. Literally, the Greek word *deceiver* (*diábolos*) means "to separate, to accuse, to give false information."[34] As Satan approached Jesus in the wilderness (Mt 4:1-11; Lk 4:1-13) he attempted to deceive him by tempting him with shortcuts to his human needs and desires – food, fame and power. Each time Jesus raised the *Shield of Faith* claiming to believe what His Father had written.

This Shield of Faith is available to me when I hear accusations about my worth and acceptability from others (or my self-thoughts). I need to look at acceptability through God's eyes. Jesus cautions us about listening to *The Devil* – the one who "is a liar and the father of lies" (Jn 8:44). In fact, Jesus claimed that *lying* is the heart language spoken by the one who slings accusations.

Paul warned the Christians to be aware of schemes presented to believers in an attempt to draw them away from their relationship with God and others (2 Cor 11:14). Satan's minions disguise themselves as *angels of light*. They have the ability to make sin look enticing and coax me to follow practices that destroy joy rather than produce joy. They show the happy crowd dancing and smiling as they drink alcohol, but they hide the broken homes and broken lives to which alcohol can lead. Satan's workers constantly accuse others in my mind so that I believe they are the problem in my life; I could not possibly be at fault. These demons work to destroy the relationships God created for me to enjoy. They attempt to show me why I need to raise a Shield of Deception rather than put my hope in God, my Shield.

Standing in God: My Shield

Unfortunately, the fiery darts of criticism are a reality in our lives. These darts will come from people who do not agree with our choices. They will be hurled by people who question our motives. Hurt and angry people will look for someone to blame. The most difficult sting will be those darts that come from friends and family members. As I feel the pain caused by their accusations, I must remember they were thrown by people seeking to protect their own acceptability by calling mine into question. Their actions result from the fear they might lose their acceptability in the eyes of others.

For this reason God provides the Shield of Faith to block the deception and accusations of the *flaming arrows of the evil one*. The Shield of Deception fails to protect my acceptability. It blocks the truth and puts my heart at war. The Shield of Faith uses the truth to block the deception. The same way Jesus used it in the wilderness, when a lie is presented, block it with the truth. When some word or action tempts me to deny my acceptability, I must believe what God says about it (Eph 1:3-6[35]). When Satan attempts to convince me that God cannot or will not help me, I choose to believe that "God is able to keep that which I have committed to him" (2 Ti 1:12). When an event happens in my life and I believe the truth will cause me to die relationally, I don't need to worry about death because Christ took my place in death (1Jn 3:16). In fact, when I accepted Christ as my savior I died. Like Paul, I can say, "I have been crucified with Christ; it is no longer I that live . . ." (Galatians 2:20). In other words, "You cannot kill me; I have died already. You cannot take away what God has given." That puts my heart at peace. There is no need for a false shield or cumbersome swords.

Strengthening My Stand in God

Prayer:

> [As you put on the armor of God and raise the Shield of Faith] Pray in the Spirit on all occasions with all kinds of prayers and requests. With this in mind, be alert and always keep on praying for all the saints. Pray also for me...
>
> ~~Ephesians 6:18-19

I find it very difficult to aim my Sword of Blame against a person for whom I am praying. Prayer not only strengthens my trust in God as my shield, it puts events into proportion so I see them through His eyes. For this reason the hymn writer encourages, "Each piece [of the gospel armor] put on with prayer."[36] As I take a position in God's refuge, I pray God will help me recognize deception and properly respond to it.

65

See The Person As God Sees Them:

If I cannot see people through God's eyes I will find fault and dehumanize them in order to justify my attack. The first lesson in this series attempted to make this point. If I see with God's eyes I will recognize all people were created in God's image (*Imago dei*) and, like me, are in need of His grace.

Through God's eyes I will recognize the true enemy and know it is not flesh and blood (another person). In fact, I will see my *opponent* as a hurting (deceived) person for whom Christ died. They are not an object or a roadblock; they are a person who has hopes, cares, needs and fears just as I do. They are simply someone responding to protect their acceptability.

I recently spoke to a businessman whose company was forced into bankruptcy by two women who embezzled more than two hundred thousand U.S. dollars. I asked him, "How do you feel toward these two women now that your business, your dream, has come to an end?" I shall never forget his response, "I see them as people who need God's grace as much as I need God's grace." Further conversation revealed that this man's trust was in God's sovereignty. Therefore, he raised the Shield of Faith and chose to set his heart at peace in the midst of a difficult situation.

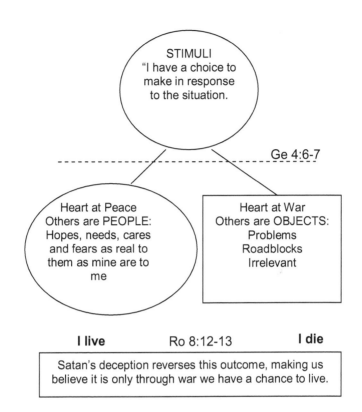

STIMULI
"I have a choice to make in response to the situation.

Ge 4:6-7

Heart at Peace
Others are PEOPLE:
Hopes, needs, cares and fears as real to them as mine are to me

Heart at War
Others are OBJECTS:
Problems
Roadblocks
Irrelevant

I live   Ro 8:12-13   **I die**

Satan's deception reverses this outcome, making us believe it is only through war we have a chance to live.

4. Two Choices

The above illustration is adapted from The Arbinger Institute's "Way-of-Being" diagram from *The Anatomy of Peace.* [37] It summarizes what I have been saying. It pictures our two choices when we perceive that our acceptability is threatened.

The top circle indicates the behavior (stimuli) that causes me to choose an action. I seldom have any control over the *behaviors* chosen by the other person/s in an encounter. I do not put the words in their mouth; I do not cause them to swing a fist; and I do not cause them to gather others to side with them. However, I must choose how I will respond to their behavior. I am only responsible for my words and actions. The dashed line in the chart indicates that short period of time between the behavior and my choice. At this point no further *damage* or *healing* has taken place.

It was at this point God came to Cain, before he crossed this dashed line, and warned him about the choice he was about to make.

> Then the LORD said to Cain, "Why are you angry? Why is your face downcast? If you do what is right, will you not be accepted? But if you do not do what is right, sin is crouching at your door; it desires to have you, but you must master it.
>
> ~~Genesis 4:6-7

"If you do what is right, will you not be accepted?" Isn't *acceptability* my heart's goal? God offers this to Cain and He offers it to us so through the right choices we will have a heart that is at peace. However, if Cain rejected God's offer, he would become mastered by the deception that would lead to sin.

A Heart at Peace[38]

In situations where I have Cain's choice, I hope to follow the Apostle Paul's advice "to take captive every thought to make it obedient to Christ" (2 Co 10:5). However, this is neither the easiest nor the common way of reacting to negative stimuli.

I struggle with the choices. The difficult decisions required to put my heart at peace often elude me. The natural reaction of my sin-based instinct demands that I protect myself. I do not want to take my thoughts captive; I want to allow them to flow and do the obvious. However, the only hope for *acceptability* or a continuing relationship with those involved resides in the choice for *peace.*

To choose peace I must understand not all conflict is bad. Much good can come from two people discussing differences with a Heart of Peace. Proverbs refers to it as, "iron sharpening iron" (Pr 27:17). Each of us brings a different heritage to the situation. We look at the same problem through different lenses − different education, different personality, different passions, etc. These differences can be the strength of our relationships and decisions. I can stand in God's protection and raise a Shield of Faith to enjoy and learn from others. Or, I can pick up my Shield of Deception, grab my Sword of Blame and attack.

To choose a *heart at peace* opens the way to God's goal of reconciliation. With my Shield of

Deception down and a hand out instead of a sword, God's plan for peace has greater possibility. Paul warns:

> For if you live according to the sinful nature, you will die; but if by the Spirit you put to death the misdeeds of the body, you will live, because those who are led by the Spirit of God are sons of God.
>
> ~~Romans 8:13-14

Paul tells the Galatians, "It is no longer I that live, but Christ in me" (Gal 2:20). Therefore, I can show vulnerability because my acceptability is no longer at risk. I have been accepted and I have an eternal home.

In the next chapter I will share guidelines for what to do if the person who has attacked refuses to accept peace. *Peace* is to be my response, *vengeance* is God's responsibility. "Be still and know that I am God" (Ps 46:10). Even when evidence convicts the other person, my actions remain my responsibility. If I choose peace, I live.

A Heart at War[39]

When I perceive someone blocking my route to acceptability my reactions call for war. I hide behind my Shield of Deception and raise my Sword of Blame to denounce them as my problem. I inflate my own virtues and devalue theirs. I sense them as *goal-blocking obstacles*. Because of this, any need, care, hope or fear they may have is irrelevant to the situation.

The choice of war presents another problem; if I choose this course of action I destroy any hope for reconciliation. Therefore, I *die* in the relationship. Satan's goal of *separation* finds reality – estrangement, divorce or death. Restoration of relationships cannot be reached from behind a Shield of Deception.

I cannot begin to solve a conflict problem until I am willing to admit that, "I am the problem." Whether I have done any wrong or not evades the reality that my *opponent* perceives that I pose a threat to their need for acceptability. Or, I perceive they are blocking mine. I might not realize how I have done so. It may have been unintentional. It does not matter. I have to accept the fact I am the problem and from that point begin to move toward peace. Author, Jim Van Yperen writes,

> [We] must be the first to own the problem. He must ask, "What is it about me that is causing this event to happen?" ... Start with the assumption that you may be a part of the problem. By asking

the question, "What is it about me that is making [this person] react in this way?"[40]

Our Choice

We all woke up this morning with a choice of two shields available to us. With one I protect my acceptability at the risk of destroying it. With the other I am protected by God's truth and shielded from deception. I cannot do battle with both shields at the same time. I must choose one or the other.

Discussion Questions

Chapter Two

1. Before the session begins, share with each other your experiences of noticing *imago dei.*

2. What do you fear the most, physical death or the death of a relationship?

3. When a conversation begins to *heat up*, do you feel the presence of two shields? If so, which seems the most useful? Why?

4. If we are tempted to raise the Shield of Deception to protect our *acceptance*, what truth does Ephesians 1:3-6 speak to this deception?

5. Discuss the two choices given Cain (Genesis 4:6-7). Are they still valid choices for us today?

Love must be sincere. Hate what is evil; cling to what is good. Be devoted to one another in brotherly love. Honor one another above yourselves. Never be lacking in zeal, but keep your spiritual fervor, serving the Lord. Be joyful in hope, patient in affliction, faithful in prayer. Share with God's people who are in need. Practice hospitality.

Bless those who persecute you; bless and do not curse. Rejoice with those who rejoice; mourn with those who mourn. Live in harmony with one another. Do not be proud, but be willing to associate with people of low position. Do not be conceited.

Do not repay anyone evil for evil. Be careful to do what is right in the eyes of everybody. If it is possible, as far as it depends on you, live at peace with everyone. Do not take revenge, my friends, but leave room for God's wrath, for it is written: "It is mine to avenge; I will repay," says the Lord ... Do not be overcome by evil, but overcome evil with good.

~~ Romans 12:9-19, 21

Chapter 3

MAINTAINING RELATIONSHIPS

How to Keep a Heart of Peace in the Time of War

It was not a verbal Sword of Blame that David had to dodge, but a physical one thrown by King Saul. The king was not happy about David's popularity. Saul determined he had to kill David to protect himself and his rule. Twice he threw a spear at David. When David escaped Saul led his army in pursuit of him. David and his followers fled from Saul's presence but never took an offensive position against him. Twice David had opportunity to kill Saul, but he would not give into a heart of war.

At one point in his exile David led a band of six hundred men. He had made a pact with Achish, King of Gath, in which the king gave David and his men the city of Ziklag as a residence for their wives and children. When the men returned to Ziklag they discovered the town had been burned. The attackers had taken the women and children captive (1 Sa 30). In their grief the men began blaming David for their loss and picked up rocks to stone him. As he had done so many times with Saul, this great warrior chose to keep his heart at peace. "David found strength in the LORD his God" (1 Sa 30:6). He understood his men's reaction and sought the Lord's guidance (1 Sa 30:8). He allowed God to be his shield and to work His plan.

David again made a choice for peace when his son Absalom led a rebellion against him. He fled the city rather than take up arms. Again he allowed God to be his shield and to work His plan. When David returned to the city Shimei, a man who had previously hurled rocks and insults against him (2 Sa 16:5-14), came and sought forgiveness. David's men did not want to allow it, but he chose peace instead of war (2 Sa 19:18-23).

In each incident, David made himself vulnerable in order to keep peace. The dictionary defines *vulnerable* as "Susceptible to attack, or open to censure or criticism."[41] It describes laying down one's shield and sword in order to prevent conflict or to make peace in the midst of discord. Even when David knew that Saul was jealous of him, he supported Saul's sovereignty. When David's men wanted to stone him, he did not defend himself. When his son rebelled, he did not fight back. In each situation he made himself vulnerable knowing God would shield him.

Vulnerability is an action, not a passive dropping of the sword and saying, "Do what you will to me." The vulnerable one stands before the enemy for the purpose of reconciliation. It might mean confessing, "I am wrong. I don't always see things correctly. Therefore, share with me what I can do to bring resolution." Vulnerability is saying, "If someone needs to die in this situation, I am willing to be that one."

Vulnerability requires me to raise the Shield of Faith rather than the Shield of Deception. With God as my protector, I believe what He has promised – He can/will help me in this situation. Therefore, I do not need to deceive myself or others. I believe the scripture gives some clear guideline about how to keep my heart at peace by remaining vulnerable. However, these actions defy the natural response of our fallen nature. I want to share four uncommon steps to maintaining peace.

1. Be Still

I sit amazed as I study scriptures dealing with handling conflict. So many times God directed His people to *be still*. Being still is the ultimate act of vulnerability. Every instinct demands *fight* or *flight*. *Self-defense, self-preservation* are the common approach to an impending battle. One student of resolving conflicts writes:

> Either party can break the cycle simply by not responding to the perceived threat ... Jesus tells us to "turn the other cheek," to "do good" and to "pray for" those who hate us. Refusing to react defensively can actually reverse

the cycle so that the energy is given to listening, learning and serving others rather than protecting self."[42]

The word *still* describes David's choice when his men threatened him – he did not take a defensive mode but rather called upon the Lord. When Shimei pelted David with insults, the king's men wanted to kill Shimei, but David, in stillness said, "Perhaps what he is saying is God's message to me" (2 Sam 16:10 paraphrase). May that be my attitude in the face of accusations.

To *be still* means to drop the shield, lay down the sword and allow God to shield you. It does not mean hiding or avoiding the situation. It means before you act, you will think through the circumstances, call upon God and await His direction.

Stillness is the lost ingredient in understanding how God can cause wars to cease. Because we are so easily deceived into action many believers remain in battle with one another. In lesson two, I read these words of David,

> He makes wars cease to the ends of the earth; he breaks the bow and shatters the [sword], he burns the shields with fire. **Be still, and know that I am God**; I

will be exalted among the nations, I will be exalted in the earth.

~~Psalms 46:9-10
(emphasis added)

The Hebrew word translated *be still* that David uses in this song stems from *raphah* – *to mend, to cure, or to heal.*[43] Is David suggesting that *stillness* can lead to *healing*? The variation used in Psalm 46 can be translated, "Be still, relax, or cease striving."[44] The only way that the God who heals (Ex 15:26) can work in my conflicts is if I remain still and allow Him to do so. My quick reactions tend to block His attempt to help.

When Moses led the people out of Egypt they found themselves pinned against the Red Sea with the Egyptian army coming against them. The people confronted Moses, blaming him for the situation. Moses remained calm and assured the Israelites that "The LORD will fight for you; **you need only to be still**" (Ex 14:14 emphasis added). The New King James Version translates *be still* as *"hold your peace."* Moses reminds the people, "God can and will handle our situation." The same is true for me; I only need to choose a heart of peace.

Job had to make this choice. When he was in the midst of his trials he struggled at keeping his heart at peace. He wanted God to come down and

79

explain Himself. Elihu counseled him to "**Stand still** and consider the wondrous works of God" (Job 37:14 NKJV emphasis added). I remember one particular time during my ministry I was having a difficult time. I asked God to show me in His Word what I should do. I closed my office door and told God that I would open my Bible and read where my finger pointed. With eyes closed, three times that morning I opened my Bible to a gospel record of Jesus' resurrection. The first two times I said, "Thank you Lord. I believe in your resurrection; but what should I do about this situation?" After the third time of reading the Resurrection Story, I heard God softly speak, "If I can raise my son from the dead, I can handle your problems." Elihu was telling Job, "If God can do these wondrous works, He can help you in your struggles." Unless I choose *stillness* I will not see and hear the wonders of God, which includes His care, His promises and His healing.

The Deceiver wants me to believe I need to react quickly. "Strike while the iron is hot." "If you wait, they will take advantage of you." Many such thoughts cross my mind. David knew this, but he testifies, "I am still confident of this; I will see the goodness of the Lord in the land of the living. **Wait for the LORD**; be strong and take heart and **wait for the LORD**" (Ps 27:13-14 emphasis added).

Paul reminds the Corinthians "love is patient" (1 Co 13:4). Immediate reactions must be controlled when relationships hang in the balance. A time of *stillness* allows us to *respond* rather than *react*. During this time of silence the following four important steps may be taken.

A New Understanding of Conflict

My first response to conflict is that something negative is happening to me. This understanding causes me to think defensively. If someone disagrees with me, criticizes me or rejects my idea, it is seen as negative and my acceptability is in jeopardy. However, not all that is labeled *conflict* should be seen as negative. It could be that God is attempting to speak into my life. I need to change my reactive reflexes so that I can respond according to what God is saying.

The Prophet Nathan risked huge conflict as he was sent by God to confront King David for his affair with Bathsheba (2 Sam 12:1). However, the Lord was using another person to speak into His leader's life. Perhaps that *criticism* from my wife, an elder or staff member that I took so hard was actually a person God was using to speak to me. Before I react to the words, I need to be silent and evaluate what was said. "Could it have been from the Lord? David thought so (2 Sam 12:13).

Marriage and leadership meetings often produce two opposing views of an issue. When this happens I feel an immediate need to justify my position and convince *the opposition* to accept my opinion. However, it might be that their view is just as credible as mine. They are looking at the situation from a different point of view – different experience, different heritage or different education. They might have information/knowledge I do not have. In quiet reflection, I need to consider the worth of the other person (they bare the image of God and have hopes, needs, cares and fears by which they make judgments – just like me). They may be saving me from a major mistake. Or, by taking into account their point of view along with my insight, there might be a convergence that will bring about a better solution for all involved.

In neither of these situations is the *conflict* to be seen as a negative. Yes, there was disagreement, but with positive results. God is not afraid to use other people to speak in to my personal life or to the organization to which I am responsible for leadership. Let's continue on to see what else I need to be doing while being still.

Search Your Heart

How do you control a very active youth group? I have a friend who found a way. As in any group there were times when conversation took a wrong direction – cutting remarks, gossip or complaining, etc. The group decided together that at such times anyone could shout out "attitude check" and everyone would have to stop and think about their words and/or actions. If they were guilty of a bad attitude they must ask for forgiveness. It worked and prevented many relationships from being permanently destroyed.

David links *stillness* to *attitude check* as he advises; "In your anger do not sin; when you are on your beds, **search your hearts and be silent**" (Psalm 4:4 emphasis added). When anger comes upon me, I lie in bed and let it stew as I think of all the wrongs the person has done to me and rehearse the words I'll return (I can be very bold while lying on my bed). However, David counsels us to reverse the thinking process and, instead of making a list of wrongs, I need to check my attitude and make sure it honors God and displays His love.

How do I rest in God as my shield? In the quiet stillness of vulnerability I, like David, check my attitude. I make sure my thinking measures to biblical guidelines for spiritual and relational health. During this time of reflection I take captive every thought and expose them to the light of Jesus' example and teaching (2 Co 10:5). In this time of heart searching there are at least three truths I need to confess.

1) "I Can Be Wrong"

David, again, provides our example. King Saul had every priest at Nob killed because they had given David food, and Ahimelech had inquired of the Lord on David's behalf. David heard about the massacre from Ahimelech's son who had escaped.

Instead of reacting to the death of his friends, David took responsibility (1Sa 22:20-22). When confronted by an angel about a plague God had sent on Judah because of an unauthorized census, David admitted it was he who should be punished, not the people (2 Sa 24:17). When Paul stood before King Agrippa to give a defense for his life, he made no excuses for his persecution of Christians; he admitted he was wrong (Ac 26:9-11).

My ability to admit my part in the problem is a big step toward vulnerability. I must be willing to own the problem. Therefore, I ask, 'What about me is causing this to happen?" Even if I do not believe that I originated the problem, something in me caused the other person to perceive me as a problem. My denial of this reality does not bring a solution. I must subdue any pride that rises to cloud the situation. Remember, "God opposes the proud but gives grace to the humble" (James 4:6). Author James Van Yepren writes:

> Assuming that you are part of the problem has another benefit, it eliminates blaming. Assigning blame is one of the great obstacles to real learning and resolution. Blame is Satan's tool to divide and conquer.[45]

2) "I Struggle with Some Life Situations"

As a pastor I could easily pray and give advice until an event hit me personally. When I received the phone call that my grandchild would be born with a bad heart, I immediately began to ask the *why questions* I had heard from people whom I had counseled during thirty years as a pastor. I struggled with why God would allow such an event into my good, God-fearing family? The next Sunday morning I shared my struggles before the congregation and asked for their prayers.

Twelve times the Psalms record their author crying out, "How long, O Lord, will you forget me." Notice David's struggle,

> How long, O LORD? Will you forget me forever? How long will you hide your face from me? How long must I wrestle with my thoughts and every day have sorrow in my heart? How long will my enemy triumph over me? Look on me and answer, O LORD my God. Give light to my eyes, or I will sleep in death.
>
> ~~Psalm 13:1-3

Because I am a fellow struggler, I do not always have the answers for the people who come to me for counsel. One of the problems Job's friends displayed was trying to give advice rather than comfort. Sometimes, instead of speaking, I cried with people in their hurt and confusion. I discovered later that such a response produced greater benefit than all the wise words I could have mustered.

I want others to offer grace and understanding when I am struggling. If I expect understanding I must understand that those who come to me with a heart of war are struggling with needs, hopes, cares and fears.

3) "I Need God's Grace"

A young man from my church approached me and said, "I feel called to be a pastor, but I know I will never be one." "Why," I asked, "do you say that?" He responded, "Because I make mistakes." I responded, "Sit down for a few minutes; I have something I need to share with you." I asked him to forgive me for giving him the impression that I do not make mistakes. (The young man did become a pastor.)

Because I make mistakes, because I struggle and because I have weaknesses I need God's grace. Without grace there would be no acceptability for me. I pray for it, I need it, I claim it. I am willing to admit I am the problem in this difficult time in my relationship with another person. I am faced with a person about whom I must choose between war and peace. In my mind they have blocked my acceptability. They challenged my leadership and have made me feel insignificant. They have said or done something that has injured my spirit. What is my response?

First, because I am a part of the problem, I need grace. I desire God's grace as well as grace from the other person/s. Next, I must realize the person with whom I am having the difficulty also needs grace. Grace has been extended to both of us by the loving heart of God, and now it is up to me to extend it to them.

People around me are all individuals who have hopes, needs, cares and fears just like I do. What they did or said was based upon their desire for acceptability, just as my response to them will be based upon my own wish for the same. In light of this, Paul's words become so important.

> Do not let any unwholesome talk come out of your mouths, but only what is helpful for building others up *according to their needs*, that it may benefit those who listen.

> ~~Ephesians 4:29
> (emphasis added)

I define *grace* as *uncommon love.* It goes beyond the limits of what the world claims as love's boundaries. Grace makes no sense to the uninformed observer. But, in order for me to call upon a God of grace, I must be willing to extend grace.

Because I can admit weaknesses, I can be open to correction and criticism. No person has ever avoided having their decisions come under scrutiny. I am criticized by people who would handle situations or express thoughts differently than I do. However, I do not need to face criticism with a heart at war. If criticism is valid, I need to make the correction. If it is invalid, I should sincerely ask forgiveness and move on. There is no need to attack the person who delivered it. If the criticism hurts, I need to raise the Shield of Faith to block any deception concerning God's ability to act and trust in what He has already said about my acceptability. I must ask God, who is willing to help in my weaknesses, to love that person through me.

In the time of stillness these thoughts should be allowed to flow through my mind. However, whether in stillness or quickness, I must deal with my natural desire to go to war. Therefore, I must take the next step beyond just being still.

Some cultures believe words are alive. Therefore, once words are spoken they cannot be retracted. If a person perceives a curse has been spoken, they will duck so the words do not strike them. If the words are a blessing, they stand in front of the speaker so the words hit them. It is this knowledge that gives me a mental picture for this point in the lesson.

I mentioned this directive earlier, but it bears repeating. As I process my thinking concerning what I perceive as impending conflict, I must remember there is a way that seems right, but it will end in death – either physical or relational death (Pr 16:25). The way that *seems right* is to attack back with equally hurting words. However, Paul reports that, "We take captive every thought to make it obedient to Christ" (2 Corinthians 10:5). My mental picture sees these war-producing thoughts as living words escaping my mind. Therefore, I reach out and grab them and bring them struggling in my hands to the truth of scripture. This response can only come as I am *being still*. It will be very difficult to capture my thinking while I am reacting.

There is a vast difference between *reacting* and *responding*. My *reactions* immediately flare with very little thought to their potential damage. *Response* follows stillness. James reminds us, "Everyone should be quick to listen, slow to speak and slow to become angry, for man's anger does not bring about the righteous life that God desires" (Jas 1:19-20). Only in the moments of *being still* can I take charge of my thoughts and hear God's plan for my situation, and that leads us to our next step in *being still*.

Listen for God

When David's men wanted to blame him for the loss of their wives and children, his first response was to remain still and listen to God (1 Sa 30:6). All through David's life I find the phrase, "inquire of the Lord." Ahimelech, confessed he had inquired of the Lord for David on several occasions (1 Sa 22:15). This phrase describes the responses of Solomon, Jehoshaphat, Josiah, Isaiah and Jeremiah; they inquired of the Lord. James promises that if I lack the wisdom for handling a given situation I "should ask God, who gives generously to all without finding fault, and it will be given . . ." (James 1:5). The writer of Proverbs instructs me to "Trust in the LORD with all your heart and lean not on your own understanding; in all your ways acknowledge him, and he will make your paths straight" (Pro 3:5-6). This can only be accomplished during a quiet time of listening.

Allow God to Act

I am prone to reaction. I have a tendency to step in front of God, blocking His plan for handling the situation. Then, after I have messed everything up, I go back to God and ask, "Where were you?" or, "Can you fix this?" Deception says, "Fight!" Truth blocks the deception reminding me God can and will help me. In stillness I open the way for His response. I am God's child; He has promised to act on my behalf. But, I must wait for Him (Isa 30:18).

The same God who stood with David and Moses walks with me. When the Israelites were backed up against the Red Sea, Moses reminded them that they only needed to be still because, "The Lord will fight for you . . ." (Exodus 14:14).

When Korah led a rebellion against Moses, rather than reacting to their challenge, Moses responded with a plan to allow God to speak (Nu 16:4-5). When David went to encounter Goliath he claimed "All those gathered here will know that it is *not by sword or spear* that the LORD saves; for the battle is the LORD's, and he will give all of you into our hands" (1 Sa 17:47 emphasis added). With our analogy of the shield and sword, David's words speak even louder.

If the situation calls for vengeance, God is better able to handle the particulars. Retaliation is God's responsibility; my assignment is to show kindness (Ro 12:14-21). I found it interesting when I turned to Leviticus 19:18 to read what Jesus called the "Second Greatest Commandment" (Mat 22:39).

It begins with instructions to not seek revenge or bear a grudge.

When I take God's responsibility for dealing with people, I am liable to make the situation worse. That is why Jesus, in His "Parable of the Weeds," tells the disciples to allow God to handle the weeds so good wheat is not lost (Mt 13:24-30). God is the Gardner, He will prune the vines as they are needed (Jn 15:1-15). I only have to stay out of His way.

I have two friends who have experienced dramatic examples of God's vengeance. One was the pastor of a large church where a man decided my friend should no longer be the leader. He hired five prostitutes to come before the congregation and accuse the pastor of employing their services. My friend knew he could not fight such a weight of evidence; therefore, he chose to hide in God and trust His deliverance. Within a week, four of the five ladies came forward and confessed to lying and asked for forgiveness. When the man who hired them was confronted by the elders, he refused to admit that he had hired the women. That night he had a heart attack. My pastor friend went to the hospital to minister to him, but the man refused to see him. The man who had hired the prostitutes died later that night.

Another pastor friend watched three men stand in front of his congregation and announce they were taking over the leadership. They told the pastor he could only preach when scheduled and on a subject they would assign. My friend came and asked my counsel. We prayed together and I advised, "Do not fight against them. Minister to them and pray for them; God will handle the situation."

The three men decided they wanted to dismiss the pastor; however, they had no authority to do so. The congregation was a new ethnic church plant that met in our building, and they relied on our elders to oversee their work until they could appoint their own. Therefore, our elders told the three men they could not terminate the pastor because, "We hired him and it is our building you are using. His leadership is our decision to make."

The three men took several people and started another church and led a campaign to take all the remaining members with them. I told my friend, "Do not fight. Keep ministering and preaching positive messages from scripture. Never speak against these men. Allow God to work His plan." About two months later one of the leaders came back to the church and, on his knees before the congregation, asked for forgiveness. The two remaining men suddenly lost their jobs and the lease on the room they used for their church meetings.

It takes strength to be able to leave the problem to God. Everything within me is screaming to take action and preserve my acceptability. "I have to be right!" "I deserve to have my rights!" "I must be in control." "I want to be heard." "I must protect myself." All these reactions *seem to be right*, but all lead to death. Only in the stillness with God as our shield is there life.

One Last Word

During one of my ministries we had a group who wanted me to resign because "instead of ministering to them, all I did was bring in new people." I refused to fight against them. After the congregation gave me a vote of confidence, one of my supporters came to me and said, "Now you have them on the run. Now is the time to show that you are the boss here." I told him I would do nothing of the kind. He reacted by saying, "I have watched you during this entire ordeal, and you have always refused to fight, even when we were willing to fight on your side. I am sorry; I cannot respect a weak person who will not fight. I am leaving this congregation." He never returned to church after that conversation.

Satan works to confuse our thinking concerning right and wrong. His goal is to separate, not allow reconciliation. He must thwart any attempt at restoration and unity. To accomplish this he attempts to convince me that power and revenge are good; any other response portrays weakness. Deceived by Satan's philosophy of power, some will accuse me of being weak because I chose a heart of peace (God's way of love and humility). In reality, it takes more strength to follow God's plan for relationships. Satan shows us a wide, easy path that leads to destruction (Mt 7:13). Although God's path is narrow and difficult, it leads to life (Mt 7:14).

Stillness covers only the first step that scripture reveals as a guideline to keeping a heart of peace in the time of war. There is still more I can do to live in peace. We will not find any of the following three steps any easier than the first. But, I have found them to work.

2. PRAISE as an Act of Obedience

Praise does not describe my normal response to difficult situations. When I perceive an attack on my acceptability, shouting *hallelujah* fails as my first reaction. When someone shoots at my character, *rejoicing* does not pass through my thoughts. However, I have to move beyond the belief that praise is an act of emotion. Even though the scriptures teach us to praise God in difficult situations, they never indicate it is a response of laughter.

> Give thanks in all circumstances,
> for this is God's will for you in
> Christ Jesus.
>
> ~~1 Thessalonians 5:18

Do not be anxious about anything, but in everything, by prayer and petition, with thanksgiving, present your requests to God.

~~Philippians 4:6

Consider it pure joy, my brothers, whenever you face trials of many kinds.

~~James 1:2

Praise is not an act of emotion; it is the surrender of my pride. It takes the focus off me and my needs and puts the focus on God. Praise helps me lift the Shield of Faith to deflect the deception of the evil one. I praise God's sovereignty. I praise Him for His unconditional love and that His promises do not sway with the opinions of others. I praise Him because He sent His son to take my place in death so I no longer need to worry about dying. I praise Him because through His son my acceptability now and forever is sealed. I praise Him because He desires to lead in the response to the current situation; it is not up to me. Finally, I praise Him because I am limited in strength and knowledge; He is not.

Praise flows from a heart filled with God's joy. Joy describes another characteristic of the Christian life that I tend to mistakenly equate with emotions. The biblical word has nothing to do with emotions. Rather, my emotions flow from my realization of God's ability to supply my true needs. It comes from knowing I already belong to Him (Jn 1:12; 1 Jn 3:1) and He will not give me a stone instead of bread (Mt 7:9). He will not allow me to be tempted beyond what I can endure (1 Co 10:13). This produces a peace that passes understanding (Php 4:7) that translates into *joy*.

English translates Jesus' Beatitudes as *Blessed* (Mt 5:1-12). I had problems with these promises until I realized Jesus was not making a future statement. He is talking about the here and now. It is not the "poor in spirit" who *will be* blessed; they *already have* God's joy. The Greek word describes an assurance my needs are met "above earthly sufferings and labors."[46] Anger is a product of deception. Peace comes through truth. Depression is the result of deception. Joy flows from truth. This joy produces a peace that results in praise.

Outside of scripture, praise becomes my single most effective weapon. It takes the focus off of me and puts it upon God – His love, sovereignty and power. Therefore, in stillness my thoughts turn to God's promises and abilities and that leads to praise. Now it is time to respond according to God's directives.

3. Obey Scriptural Principles

Put on a Gentle Spirit

Paul's counsel to Timothy is a message that needs no commentary:

> Flee the evil desires of youth, and pursue righteousness, faith, love and peace, along with those who call on the Lord out of a pure heart. Don't have anything to do with foolish and stupid arguments, because you know they produce quarrels. And the Lord's servant must not quarrel; instead, he must **be kind** to everyone, able to teach, not resentful. Those who oppose him he must **gently** instruct, in the hope that God will grant them repentance leading them to a knowledge of the truth, and that they will come to their senses and escape from the trap of the devil, who has taken them captive to do his will.
>
> ~~2 Timothy 2:22-26
> (emphasis added)

God's instructions to *gentleness* are consistent, I cannot deny them.

A **gentle** answer turns away wrath, but a harsh word stirs up anger.

~~Proverbs 15:1
(emphasis added)

Let your **gentleness** be evident to all. The Lord is near.

~~Philippians 4:5
(emphasis added)

Be completely humble and **gentle**; be patient, bearing with one another in love.

~~Ephesians 4:2
(emphasis added)

But the fruit of the Spirit is love, joy, peace, patience, kindness, goodness, faithfulness, **gentleness** and self-control. Against such things there is no law.

~~Galatians 5:22-23
(emphasis added)

The Greek word chosen in these passages means *mild and gentle friendliness*.[47] Thus, we have a description of what our response is to trouble.

Seek Reconciliation -- Matthew 18:15-17

Did you ever throw your Bible at God? I did. I had a staff member who was caught in sin. I was angry with him. I wanted to yell at him and make him feel my fury. The morning I was to confront him I went to my office for a quiet time of prayer. I was reading through Galatians at the time and turned to that morning's passage:

> Brothers, if someone is caught in a sin, you who are spiritual should restore him **gently**. But watch yourself, or you also may be tempted.
>
> ~~Galatians 6:1
> (emphasis added)

In anger I yelled, "No, I won't do it!" and threw my Bible across the room and it smashed against a bookshelf. I sat and stared into the morning light for about ten minutes, got up, picked up my Bible and asked, "Okay, how do you want me to handle this?" God outlined a plan for reconciliation and restoration.

Scripture gives no relief to my desire for the offender to call me and ask for my forgiveness. Jesus says very clearly if I become aware of someone who sees me as their problem, I am to go to that person. My flesh says, "Those words in the Sermon on the Mount do not apply to this situation. Besides, the first principle in these lessons is to wait. So, wait for them to make the first move." However, that is not what Jesus says.

> Therefore, if you are offering your gift at the altar and there remember that your brother has something against you; leave your gift there in front of the altar. First go and be reconciled to your brother; then come and offer your gift.
>
> ~~Matthew 5:23-24

Well, then, if I have to go to the angered person when they are the problem, then when I make a mistake should I wait for them to come me? After all, if I have to go first when they are the problem, shouldn't they have to come first when I am the problem? I have found God does not reason my way. Once again, I am directed to go first, whether I perceive the other person is the problem or I am the problem.

Matthew 18:15-17 is an excellent outline for what to do when having difficulty with another person.

> If your brother sins against you, go and show him his fault, just between the two of you. If he listens to you, you have won your brother over. But if he will not listen, take one or two others along, so that every matter may be established by the testimony of two or three witnesses. If he refuses to listen to them, tell it to the church; and if he refuses to listen even to the church, treat him as you would a pagan or a tax collector.
>
> ~~Matthew 18:15-17

Here, Jesus instructs us to approach the other party with shield and sword down. If a person does not respond to my first attempt for reconciliation then I am to go with a neutral party.

During my years in the pastoral ministry I have learned how easy it is to misuse Matthew eighteen. It is a guideline to reconciliation, not a formula to prove my spirituality. I have been guilty of proudly quoting this passage with my Shield of Deception raised high and my Sword of Blame pointed at the person whom I visited, "They wronged me. I went to them and they did not repent when confronted. I did what scripture told me to do. I am the spiritual one. Now I can wash my hands of the situation."

If I do this, I am guilty of *using* scripture, not *following* scripture. Jesus makes *reconciliation* the goal – "you have gained a brother" (Mt 18:15). Even if the problem is "his fault," I must confront him with a gentle and humble spirit; willing to admit any role I had in causing it.

Yes, there are times when confrontation, correction and warning are necessary. However, I must take to heart the instructions of Paul to Timothy, "command certain men not to teach false doctrines any longer ... The goal of this command is love, which comes from a pure heart and a good conscience and a sincere faith" (1 Tim 1:3-5). Even when I discern the need to correct, I am to do it with a heart of peace. I cannot get around it.

Following the counsel of author James Van Yperen, I have found the question, "Why?" works in these situations. According to Van Yperen, I should be willing to ask it four different times. Each time saying, "This is what I heard you saying; can you share with me why you see this as a problem?" He goes on. The first *why* will give me a *surface answer* dealing with symptoms. The second *why* will produce an answer dealing with the way *things* were handled. The third *why* will get an answer dealing with relationships. If a theological or scriptural misunderstanding caused the problem, the fourth

103

why will expose it. "The purpose of asking questions is to clarify the issue in order to discover the solution. Don't stop at the first answer. Most problems have little or nothing to do with the event that reveals them."[48] Even if I do not understand the core issue of the problem, I must go to the next step.

Seek to Forgive or Ask Forgiveness

I have made mistakes in my ministry and as a father – errors in judgment, failure to act or I acted inappropriately, etc. My first reaction in such situations was to raise my shield to protect myself. "I was busy, under stress." "I was justified; he must have been doing something wrong." "Pass the blame; deflect the sword; save yourself." However, such responses never lead to reconciliation.

The Lord teaches us forgiveness opens the way to healing. This is difficult but true. When I obediently go to a person and ask for forgiveness, most of the time it not only heals, it strengthens a relationship. An added blessing falls on people who look upon a Christian as a person who never makes mistakes. When I admit to wrongs, it gives them hope to grow past theirs.

> For if you forgive men when they sin against you, your heavenly Father will also forgive you. But if you do not forgive men their sins,

your Father will not forgive your sins.

~~Matthew 6:14-15

Be kind and compassionate to one another, forgiving each other, just as in Christ God forgave you.

~~Ephesians 4:32

4. MOVE ON!

Jared was a young father in the congregation where I served. He had grown up in a pastor's family. He lost a child to cancer and became very bitter and aimed his bitterness at me. No matter how many times I visited him and his wife, no matter how many times I asked for forgiveness for the unexplained problem, I could never get to the reason he disliked me so much. I finally had to say, "Before the throne of God I have done everything scripture and my elders have asked me to do. I must move on."

When I was studying to become a pastor, my mentor told me I would never be able to make everyone happy. I truly thought in my heart I would be able to prove him wrong. I was going to be different and everyone would like me and follow my leadership. Needless to say, that thinking produced some problems of its own, especially when I found myself afraid to move ahead as a leader for fear of making someone unhappy. I can still remember the day in my first year of ministry when I admitted to myself, "I cannot do it. There is no way to please everyone or to get everyone on board for the direction the church needs to go." It was a hard lesson to grasp but one I needed to learn in order to become the leader God and His people needed.

My experience was no different than what Paul faced during his ministry. In light of it he directed, "If it is possible, as far as it depends on you, live at peace with everyone" (Ro 12:18, c.f. 14:19). No matter what Paul tried, there were people who refused to be at peace with him. I have to accept that fact; there are/will be people who will refuse my overtures of peace. No matter what I do, they will continue to keep their shields raised and swords pointed at me. I cannot make their decision for them. However, I must respond according to the biblical principles I have shared in these lessons. I want to set as a goal Paul's words before Felix; "I strive always to keep my conscience clear before God and man" (Ac 24:16). And, I must do this without any spiritual pride as I move on in service to the Lord.

Nevertheless, I cannot allow the fear of someone's anger stop me from leading people to where God wants them to be. I am once again reminded of the Israelites backed up against the Red Sea with the Egyptian army coming behind them. The Israelites attacked Moses and accused him of misleading them. Moses told them God would fight the battle for them, and they only needed to be still; then God said, "Quit crying about it; move on!" (Ex 14:15 author's paraphrase).

When I cannot bring resolution to a conflict I must make a decision, set my boundaries and move on. I do not believe God wants me to allow someone to walk over me. I am not talking about co-dependency where my refusal to act empowers someone's dysfunction. I strongly disagree with those who tell a battered wife to go back to her husband and be obedient.[49] God does not expect me to become someone's personal punching bag – physically or verbally.

Clearly, *obedience* is what God wants. I must not allow my fear of losing acceptability stop my growth, or block my answering God's call on my life. Many people and organizations have come to a complete halt for fear of offending someone or because someone threatens displeasure. What truly blocks my progress is a stand, with the Shield of Deception raised high, believing God cannot or will not handle this situation. Holding my ground, I have my Sword of Blame pointed at the person(s) who I believe caused the stoppage. Only Satan wins when hearts go to war.

When honest differences exist after the process has clarified the issues, we must make the call by faith. This may result in one of at least three positive outcomes if I act wisely and humbly:

1. The two sides may separate peaceably, as did Paul and Barnabas.
2. The two sides may reach a compromise, agreeing to disagree on nonessential matters or each giving up some area of concern for the sake of unity while respecting the other's convictions.
3. One side may voluntarily remove its protest, allowing the other to move ahead.

Each of these decisions can be reached and carried out with a heart at peace.

CONCLUSION

> ### The Goal in Conflict Resolution is RECONCILIATION

Joy in our Christian walk only takes place within good relationships and only a heart of peace builds good relationships. In any relationship there will be times of difficulty. A heart of peace does not mean an absence of conflict. The closer we work/live together, the more I will become aware of your differences and you of mine. Not all conflict is bad. We learn and grow through the sharing of differences. The best relationships I have experienced are ones in which I endured struggles.

Nonetheless, these struggles were only smoothed when I developed a heart of peace.

If I am in a conflict situation, my first responsibility is to **be reconciled** with that person (Mt 5:24). This is top priority for a believer. I will not likely bring people into the Kingdom of Heaven through a heart at war. I will only succeed in alienating the person with whom I am in conflict as well as all those observing.

Reconciliation is God's goal for all. This is why He sent Jesus as an ambassador and sacrifice.

> For God was pleased to have all his fullness dwell in him, and through him to **reconcile** to himself all things, whether things on earth or things in heaven, by making peace through his blood, shed on the cross. Once you were alienated from God and were enemies in your minds because of your evil behavior. But now he has **reconciled you** by Christ's physical body through death to present you holy in his sight, without blemish and free from accusation.
>
> ~~Colossians 1:19 – 22
> (emphasis added)

109

His purpose was to create in himself one new man out of the two, thus making peace, and in this one body **to reconcile** both of them to God through the cross, by which he put to death their hostility.

~~Ephesians 2:15-16
(emphasis added)

And the God of all grace, who called you to his eternal glory in Christ, after you have suffered a little while, will himself restore you and make you strong, firm and steadfast. To him be the power for ever and ever. Amen.

~~1 Peter 5:10-11

I opened this third lesson by speaking of vulnerability and defining it as an action. In my life and ministry conflict is inevitable. I must not allow it to stop me from being what God called me to be. When I experience conflict I have a choice. I can face conflict with my fleshly nature by raising the Shield of Deception and mustering my personal power and go to war. In doing so, my goal will be to protect myself so I remain acceptable in the sight of my chosen audience. To do this I will attack the person/s by pointing the Sword of Blame at them or deflect blame to another. However, God told Cain he had two choices (Ge 4:7) and I have the same two – acceptability or alienation – war or peace.

Seeing people through God's eyes is the first essential to a heart of peace. When situations challenge our relationships we must remember, "The goal of confrontation is always gentle restoration, always health, never harm. Blame is man's way, not God's."[50] The alternative to blame places me in God's care, allowing His truth to block any deception. In humility I must maintain a heart of peace and seek reconciliation. In the stillness I listen for God's plan and allow Him to work.

The Psalmist David was one of the most vulnerable of all God's leaders. He endured more attacks and criticisms than most of us will ever face. However, I never see him with a Shield of Deception. He cries out to God. He awaits God's voice as he turns his heart to praise. He can truly be described as having a "heart at peace." Because of his trust in God to handle his situation, he sings, "I will lie down and sleep in peace, for you alone, O LORD, make me dwell in safety" (Ps 4:8). May you also sleep well.

EPILOGUE

I fear you might think that I, because I have written this series of lessons, I have command of everything mentioned here. Let me assure you that I, along with the Apostle Paul, have a long way to go in handling my initial reactions to conflict.

> Not that I have already obtained all this, or have already been made perfect, but I press on to take hold of that for which Christ Jesus took hold of me. Brothers, I do not consider myself yet to have taken hold of it. But one thing I do: Forgetting what is behind and straining toward what is ahead, I press on toward the goal to win the prize for which God has called me heavenward in Christ Jesus.
>
> ~~Philippians 3:12-14

Let us lay down our deceptive shield, throw away our blaming sword and allow God to be our refuge as we build strong relationships that lead to the healing and joy of the Christian experience; and to sleep in peace.

DEFINING QUESTION:

Are my words and actions

leading to separation or reconciliation;

will they result in Joy and Healing?

(For chapter three discussion
questions, please turn to
the following page)

Discussion Questions

Chapter Three

1. Discuss Psalms 46:9 – 10 in light of "being still."

2. When we are willing to confess, "I am the problem," how does it affect our *acceptability*?

3. Discuss the concept, "I need grace, I must give grace."

4. Why do we find it so difficult to *move on* when someone refuses to be at peace with us?

5. How have these three lessons impacted your thinking about relationships?

APPENDIX A

Biblical Model

for

Conflict Resolution

Biblical Model for Conflict Resolution
Robert D. Kuest, D.Min.

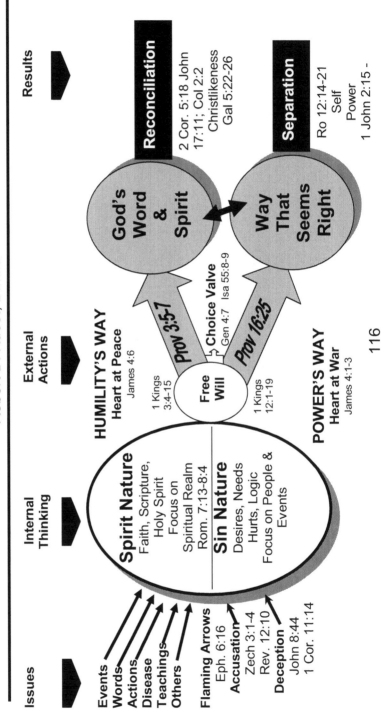

Issues

Events
Words
Actions
Disease
Teachings
Others

Flaming Arrows
Eph. 6:16
Accusation
Zech 3:1-4
Rev. 12:10
Deception
John 8:44
1 Cor. 11:14

Internal Thinking

Spirit Nature
Faith, Scripture, Holy Spirit
Focus on Spiritual Realm
Rom. 7:13-8:4

Sin Nature
Desires, Needs, Hurts, Logic
Focus on People & Events

External Actions

HUMILITY'S WAY
Heart at Peace
James 4:6

1 Kings 3:4-15

Free Will

1 Kings 12:1-19

POWER'S WAY
Heart at War
James 4:1-3

Prov 3:5-7
Choice Valve
Gen 4:7 Isa 55:8-9
Prov 16:25

God's Word & Spirit

Way That Seems Right

Results

Reconciliation
2 Cor. 5:18 John 17:11; Col 2:2
Christlikeness
Gal 5:22-26

Separation
Ro 12:14-21
Self
Power
1 John 2:15 -

116

HUMILITY'S WAY
Heart at Peace
James 4:6

1. Be Still
Ex 14:14
Ps 4:4
Ps 46:9-10
1 Co 13:4
Eph 4:1-3
Gal 5:2
Js 1:18-26

2. Praise
1 Th 5:18
Phil 4:4,8
Js 1:2

3. Obey
Mt 5:22-25
Mt 18:15-17
Eph 4:22-32
Ro 12:19-21
2 Ti 2:22-26

4, Move On
Ex 14:15
Ro 12:18
Ro 14:19

The person who chooses humility will always be accused of being weak. But, so was Jesus.

God's Word & Spirit

POWER'S WAY
Heart at War
James 4:1-3

"I have to be right!"
"I deserve to have my rights!"
"I am the leader!"
"I want to be heard."
"I will not allow this to happen to me again."
"I will get even."
"I will prove who is to blame."
"I demand loyalty."

Power cannot be proven wrong
Power cannot allow mistreatment
Power must show control
Power must have the last word
Power will justify position/actions
Power aims at revenge
Power must point to someone else
Power forces people to choose sides

Way That Seems Right

SOURCE LIST

American Heritage Talking Dictionary, 3rd ed, (1994). Cambridge, Eng: Softkey Intl., Inc.

Arbinger Institute, The. *(2002). Leadership and Self-Deception: Getting out of the Box.* San Francisco, CA: Berrett-Koehler Publishers, Inc.

Arbinger Institute, The. *(2006). The Anatomy of Peace*: *Resolving the Heart of Conflict.* San Francisco, CA: Berrett-Koehler Publishers, Inc., a BK Life book.

Arndt, William F. & Gingrich, F. Wilbur (1963). *A Greek-English Lexicon of the New Testament and other Early Christian Literature.* Chicago, IL: The University of Chicago Press.

Forester, W. (1985). Diabolos, In Gerhard Kittel & Gerhard Friedrich (eds). Geoffrey Bromiley, (trans), *Theological Dictionary of the New Testament*, Abridged in One Volume. Grand Rapids, MI: William B. Eerdmans Publishing Co.

Goldman, Burt. "Improving Interpersonal Relationships." Self Growth.com: The Online Self-Improvement Encyclopedia. Retrieved April 13, 2009 from http://www.selfgrowth.com/articles/Goldman4.html .

Hesiod (N.D.) "The Theogony." In *Hesiod, the Homeric Hymns and Homerica*. Hugh H. Evelyn-White (trans). (1936). Cambridge, Eng: Loeb Classical Library, Harvard University Press.

Kuest, Robert. (2006). *Uncommon Leadership: Servant Leadership in a Power-Based World*. Enumclaw, WA: Pleasant Word Publishers, div of Wine Press Publishing.

McGee, Robert S. (1990).*The Search for Significance*. 2nd ed. Houston, TX: Rapha Publishing.

Powell, John. (1969). *Why Am I Afraid to Tell You Who I Am?* Niles, IL: Argus Communications.

Sande, Ken. (2003). *The Peacemaker: A Biblical Guide to Resolving Personal Conflicts*. Grand Rapids, MI: Baker Book House.

Smalley, Gary. (2007). *The DNA of Relationships: Discover How You Are Designed for Satisfying Relationships*. Carol Stream, TX: Tyndale House Publishers, Inc.

Solomon, Charles. (1984). Cassette recording. "The Fear of Rejection." Denver, CO.

Van Yperen, James. (197). "Conflict: The Refining Fire of Leadership," In Barna, George (ed.), *Leaders on Leadership*, "The Leading Edge Series." Ventura, CA: Regal Books, div of Gospel Light.

ENDNOTES

ENDNOTES:

[1] Gary Smalley. *The DNA of Relationships: Discover How You Are Designed for Satisfying Relationships*. (Carol Stream: Tyndale House Publishers, Inc, 2007), p. 3.

[2] The distinction between seeing others as people or as objects is a key idea in the work of The Arbinger Institute. See: *Leadership and Self-Deception: Getting out of the Box* (San Francisco: Berrett-Koehler Publishers, Inc., 2002) and *The Anatomy of Peace: Resolving the Heart of Conflict* (San Francisco: Berrett-Koehler Publishers, Inc., a BK Life book, 2006).

[3] This study can be found in my book, *Uncommon Leadership: Servant Leadership in a Power-Based World*. (Enumclaw, WA: Pleasant Word Publishers, div of Wine Press Publishing, 2006).

[4] Hesiod, "The Theogony" in *Hesiod, the Homeric Hymns and Homerica*. Trans. Hugh H. Evelyn-White (Cambridge: Loeb Classical Library, Harvard University Press, 1936), 507-606.

[5] I have been amazed at the number of times people have shared with me that the history of their country was the same – a conquering people annihilating and/or pushing indigenous people into controlled spaces.

[6] Stuart Hamlin. Downloaded from http://www.lyricsmode.com/lyrics/r/ray_price/how_big_is_go d.html on June 9, 2010.

[7] Documentation lost.

[8] Burt Goldman. "Improving Interpersonal Relationships." Downloaded from

http://www.selfgrowth.com/articles/Goldman4.html on April 13, 2009.

[9] John Powell. *Why Am I Afraid to Tell You Who I Am?* (Niles: Argus Communications, 1969).

[10] Charles Solomon, "The Fear of Rejection." Cassette tape. Recorded in Denver, CO, 1984.

[11] "From life's outset, I find ourselves on the prowl, searching to satisfy some inner, unexplained yearning. my hunger causes us to search for people who will love us. my desire for acceptance pressures us to perform for the praise of others. I strive for success, driving my minds and bodies harder and farther, hoping that because of my sweat and sacrifice, others will appreciate us more." Robert S. McGee. *The Search for Significance.* 2nd ed. (Houston: Rapha Publishing, 1990), 11.

[12] Ibid.

[13] Ibid.

[14] *Anatomy of Peace,* 30.

[15] Jim Van Yperen, "Conflict: The Refining Fire of Leadership," *Leaders on Leadership*, "The Leading Edge Series", George Barna, ed. (Ventura: Regal Books, div of Gospel Light, 1997) 247

[16] *Leadership and Self-Deception*, vii – viii.

[17] Adapted from *Leadership and Self-Deception*, 70.

[18] *Self-betrayal* is a concept that is central in the work of the Arbinger Institute. See *Leadership and Self-Deception* and *The Anatomy of Peace.*

[19] The concept of *self-justifying images* is described in *Leadership and Self-Deception*, 81-90.

[20] Ibid. 86.

[21] Ibid.

[22] Van Yperen, 244

[23] "The Slippery Slope of Conflict," http.www.Peacemakers.net.

[24] Sande, Ken. *The Peacemaker: A Biblical Guide to Resolving Personal Conflicts*. Grand Rapids: Baker Book House, 2003.

[25] *Leadership and Self-Deception, 64.*

[26] Ibid. 92.

[27] Ibid. 125.

[28] William F. Arndt & F. Wilbur Gingrich, *A Greek-English Lexicon of the New Testament and other Early Christian Literature*. (Chicago: The University of Chicago Press, 1963), 453.

[29] See *Leadership and Self-Deception*, 51, 93-98 and *The Anatomy of Peace*, 48, where *collusion* is defined as, "A conflict where the parties are inviting the very things they're fighting against." For a deeper understanding of the concept of *collusion*, I would suggest that one study the chapters on "The Pattern of Conflict" and "Escalation."

[30] *Anatomy of Peace*, 48.

[31] *American Heritage Talking Dictionary*, 3rd ed, (Cambridge: Softkey Intl., Inc., 1994).

[32] The "Cycle of War" diagram is adapted from The Arbinger Institute's *Collusion* diagram, *Leadership and Self-Deception*, 94 & 95 and The *Anatomy of Peace*, 46 - 47.

[33] "To be or act as an adversary, resist, oppose" From the primary root, "to attack' or "to accuse." http://www.studylight.org/lex/heb/view.cgi?number=07853, downloaded, 01-15-2007. (Studylight uses the Brown-Driver-Briggs Hebrew Dictionary).

[34] W. Forester, Diabolos, *Theological Dictionary of the New Testament*, Abridged in One Volume, Gerhard Kittel & Gerhard Friedrich, eds. Geoffrey Bromiley, trans. (Grand Rapids: William B. Eerdmans Publishing Co, 1985) 150-151.

[35] "Praise be to the God and Father of my Lord Jesus Christ, who has blessed us in the heavenly realms with every spiritual blessing in Christ, for he chose us in him before the creation of the world to be holy and blameless in his sight. In love he predestined us to be adopted as his sons through Jesus Christ, in accordance with his pleasure and will — to the praise of his glorious grace, which he has freely given us in the One he loves" (Eph 1:3-6 NIV).

[36] George Duffield, Jr, "Stand Up Stand Up for Jesus", Public Domain.

[37] *The Anatomy of Peace,* 30.

[38] Note "Peace in Wartime", *The Anatomy of Peace, 20-27.*

[39] Ibid. 30.

[40] Van Yperen, 250-251.

[41] American Heritage Electronic Dictionary.

[42] Van Yperen, p. 245.

[43] James S. Strong. *Strong's Exhaustive Concordance.*

[44] Strong's Exhaustive Concordance - A primitive root; to *slacken* (in many applications, literally or figuratively):— abate, cease, consume, draw [toward evening], fail, (be) faint, be (wax) feeble, forsake, idle, leave, let alone (go, down), (be) slack, stay, be still, be slothful, (be) weak (-en).

[45] Van Yepren, p. 251.

[46] Kittel, Gerhard (Hrsg.) ; Bromiley, Geoffrey William (Hrsg.) ; Friedrich, Gerhard (Hrsg.): *Theological Dictionary of the*

New Testament. electronic ed. Grand Rapids, MI :
Eerdmans, 1964-c1976, S. 4:362.

[47] Kittel, Gerhard (Hrsg.) ; Bromiley, Geoffrey William (Hrsg.) ;
Friedrich, Gerhard (Hrsg.): *Theological Dictionary of the
New Testament.* electronic ed. Grand Rapids, MI :
Eerdmans, 1964-c1976, S. 6:646

[48] Van Yepren, ...

[49] Church leaders who counsel battered wives to go home
and be more obedient are quick to quote the first half of
Malachi 2:16, ""I hate divorce," says the LORD God of
Israel. " However, they ignore the second half of the verse,
"and I hate a man's covering himself with violence as well
as with his garment." The NIV footnotes that "covering
himself" could be translated, "covering his wife." God hates
domestic violence.

[50] Van Yperen, p 251

8594968R0

Made in the USA
Charleston, SC
25 June 2011